D1744111

LOOPS 4 LIFE

Foreword by Stephen C. Lundin, Ph.D.,
bestselling coauthor of *FISH!*

LOOPS 4 LIFE

The Progression of Success and Secret Loops to
True Happiness in Your Personal and Professional Lives

Garret Garrels and Nick Milodragovich with Mike Chaet, Ph.D.

"This book gives us a model that we can put into action right now."
Coach Mike Van Diest
Five-time Football National Champion, two-time National Coach of the Year

ISBN: 978-1456459093

Loops Publication's books are available at special quantity discounts to use as premiums and sales promotions, or for use in corporate training programs. To contact a representative, send an email inquiry to books@loops4biz.com.

Library of Congress Cataloging-In-Publication Data

Garrels, Garret. Milodragovich, Nick. Chaet, Mike.
Loops 4 Life: The Progression of Success and Secret Loops to True Happiness in Your Personal and Professional Lives

Editor: Tom Crnich

Printed in the United States of America

We dedicate this book to those individuals who are searching

for a deeper meaning in life, and who continually strive to

always *Progress their Success.*

CONTENTS

FORWARD

I will always remember the day Mike Chaet, my co-author on the book *Loops*, first used the term loops in a conversation with me. I wasn't surprised, Mike was a serial innovator, but I was fascinated by the simplicity of it. Earlier that day I was pondering the idea that "relationships are built one conversation at a time," so the jump to the idea that "success in business is accomplished by closing one loop at a time" was an easy one to make. Mike already had a manuscript and together we eventually published *Loops: Seven Keys to Small Business Success*.

When we finished *Loops*, I was drawn to another book project I had put on hold, but Mike continued to speak about *Loops* and further develop the concept. At the annual meeting of Club Management Systems Mike introduced me to Garret and Nick, developers of Pink Gloves Boxing, a fitness-boxing program for women. These guys are people that you remember because of their enthusiasm for life. Later, Mike told me that Garret and Nick had taken the Loops concept and applied it to life in a more general way. It was only a few months later and I was looking at an early version of the book you have in front of you.

As you are now aware, I communicate in stories and it only takes one more story to conclude this forward and my motivation for writing it. Fast-forward to Australia where I am teaching a class called *Responsible Leadership* to an international group of mid-career MBA students. As their final project, I asked them to develop a personal mission statement, life goals, and a personal leadership competency model. Not surprisingly, many of their life goals relate to fitness, nutrition and career accomplishment. A few of these students asked if I had any ideas or tools they might use and I introduced the *goalOgram* found in this book. It was an instant success and I continue to get emails from students thanking me for the gift. And for that I thank Garret and Nick.

So those are my stories. As you work your way around the *goalOgram* you will find your confidence increasing with every step. As you read the accompanying story, you will find the inspiration you need to keep closing life's loops. And one thing I know for sure is that you will frequently find yourself in an unanticipated state we refer to as happiness. I wish you well in your journey.

Stephen C. Lundin, Ph.D.,
Bestselling coauthor of FISH!

How It All Began

In the spring of 2006, I met Garret for the first time when he transferred to Carroll College and joined our football team. The Fighting Saints had won four straight NAIA National Championships, and we were seeing a few extra transfers that subsequent spring. Garret was a strong middle linebacker, who looked like Hulk Hogan (bandana, glasses and fu manchu included), and I was eager to see his capabilities.

Near the end of the spring semester, my positive impression of Garret went away after a misunderstanding arose a during a Friday night party. The very next night, Garret found himself in a scuffle that led to his right arm being lacerated, severing his radial artery and ulnar nerve, causing him to lose eight pints of blood. He barely survived.

What happened next was a complete turn-around. While maintaining his playful and humorous personality, Garret developed into a balanced person and valuable teammate. Looking back, Garret said,

> "It took a rock-bottom moment, for me, to realize that a person needs to define guiding principles in all realms of life. From that day forward, I vowed not only to eliminate hypocrisy in my life, but also to help others reach awareness without facing similar situations."

After a triumphant finish to my collegiate football career winning the 2007 NAIA National Championship, I began a career as a Civil Engineer while remaining at Carroll College as an assistant coach.

Not long after, I realized I was in the wrong profession. Four years of college was not enough time for me to figure out that little detail! During any free time I could muster between engineering and coaching, I vigorously studied athletic training philosophies along with researching diet and nutrition. During this time, Garret and I began talking about training methods. Every time I learned something new, I would share it with Garret. Usually, he had already read it and would then recommend another text for me to research.

Along the way, I accompanied Garret to several meetings with his mentor Dr. Mike Chaet. A few years prior, Dr. Chaet helped Garret define many decisions regarding his life goals. He gave us business guidance while introducing us to his creation: the loopOgram.

Shortly thereafter, we started a business around training athletes, in the mental game as well as the physical. This partnership led to the creation of Better Athletic Development, Inc.

After several successful training camps, Garret invited me to help train a group of women in his hometown of Anaconda,

Montana. The group called themselves Pink Gloves Boxing (PGB).

After a few weeks of helping out, Garret asked if I wanted to join his PGB business as Co-Owner. At first, I was reluctant because I knew Pink Gloves Boxing was his baby. Finally, I chose to jump in with both feet and make PGB my baby as well.

We have continued to grow our friendship and business by finding ways to help others and keeping an open mind. With that said, the loopOgram has been an integral part of our success. Seeing the need to help those we love, our friends, and our contemporaries; we were compelled to write this book.

Nick Milodragovich

THE WARM-UP

This is more than a sports book, more than a goals book, more than a business book; this is a book about closing those important loops while co-creating a successful and fulfilling life. It's the perfect primer for those looking to gain motivation and wisdom. It's the perfect foundation for those who wish to prevent falling into the traps that could ruin potentially amazing athletic, artistic, and business careers; and truly fulfilling lives. Athletes, artists, business owners, teachers, kids, and parents seeking to be their best and to inspire their teammates, fans, coworkers, and family will find many of the answers they seek within this book.

At the same time, this is not a miracle book. It would go against our credo to say this book contains all the answers to the mysteries of our existence. Nor is it a Get-Rich-Quick book; there are plenty of those already available on the market. Our *Progression of Success* (PoS) teachings can only outline the principles, behaviors, and habits necessary for success; you still need to take action. Only you can achieve personal success and only you can prevent it.

Keep in mind as you learn the principles of goal setting, you are only halfway there. You must *apply* those principles into *Goal-Getting*™ and *Loop Closing*! There is nothing more poignant in today's society, than the dreamer who dreams magnificent ideas on the couch, exclaiming: "What if *this*?" and "What if *that?*" only to turn on the TV and to allow those dreams to drift away.

The greatest enemy of courage is not cowardice; it's complacency. You must *do* today what you *want* tomorrow. Along with outlining the principles, behaviors, and habits for a fulfilling life, Our *Progression of Success* will provide you with the needed boost to propel you off the couch, and into action in pursuit of your dreams.

Collegiate students and athletes often struggle with their transition from dorm life into the *Real World*. There are few practical application classes in our universities today that provide students with a fighting chance.

As students graduate from college or high school, they go through a ceremony called *'Commencement'* which doesn't signify the end of the student's path but rather the beginning! In the next stage of life, formal education gives way to self-education. Most problems arise when those habits of self-education have never been developed. Instead of striding confidently during *'Commencement,'* many graduates feel lost, helpless, and without personal drive.

This book will help bridge the gap in the learning process, and create *Life-Long Learners and Loop Closers*; people who continually *Progress Their Success*!

LOOPS 4 *YOUR* LIFE

You will be asked to **STOP** several times throughout the book. During that time, we encourage you to take the key principles and apply them to your life. In a few words or sentences, personalize the lesson by writing in your **LOOPS 4 *YOUR* LIFE** section.

Chapter 1

STUCK IN A RUT

"The path of least resistance and least trouble is a mental rut already made. It requires troublesome work to undertake the alteration of old beliefs." John Dewey

"The only difference between a rut and a grave are the dimensions." Ellen Glasgow

It was 7:45 A.M. and Ward reluctantly crawled out of bed. As his cold feet touched the ground, the alarm sounded from his mother's mouth, "Ward, are you up yet? I've called you five times, and you're late again!" When he sleepwalked to the bathroom, Ward couldn't bring himself to answer. "Ward Jacob Young, I am not going to be happy if I have to come up there."

He met his mother halfway down the stairs. "If I hadn't threatened you out of bed, you would have missed your test this morning. How are you ever going to make it on your own if I always have to take care of you?"

"You know, Joyce," Ward replied, "if you play football in college, all you have to do is play well on Saturdays. They have people help you through school."

His mother rolled her eyes, took a deep breath and replied, "I prefer you call me 'mom', and you are in for a rude awakening. I want you to focus on your test today. It would really help your father and I if you could get some academic money because Carroll College is expensive, and they don't give 'full rides' for sports."

Coach Van Nest's major concern while recruiting Ward was his grades. Though the Fighting Saints had won five National Championships, he couldn't have led a bunch of meatheads. Despite Ward's considerably low G.P.A., Coach saw something deeper in him. He saw an undiscovered intelligence. Coach has been around long enough to know that the mark of a good leader isn't finding the best people but bringing the best out of people. A person learns this skill quickly when coaching a smaller division team. Higher divisions pick up most of the 'already hatched' athletes before anyone else even gets a chance.

Ward walked into the house and sprawled out on the couch. "Well, how did it go?" his father, Jarrod, prodded.

"I don't know, Dad, I just want to be finished with high school. I hate school, and I can't wait until football season starts."

Ward's father moved his dirty shoes from the couch and sat next to him. "I understand that you have this tunnel vision and can't wait until the season starts. Nevertheless, if you always live your life in the future, you will miss the present. If you really want to be the best football player, you have to be the best person, in all areas."

Ward tossed his dad the remote, nodded and went into his room. He thought to himself, "They just don't get it. Lawrence Taylor never had to worry about school or work. He also had a lot of drug problems." He began to analyze his situation a little deeper, "Maybe that's not the best example. Maybe there is more to a successful life than just football." Just then, the phone interrupted his thoughts.

"Pete's Pizza Place." He answered thinking it was one of his friends.

"Umm...Is Ward Young there?" There was no mistaking Coach Van Nest's tone. His voice was very clear; as distinct as a purple cow.

"Hey, Coach. Sorry, I thought you were one of my friends," Ward sheepishly said as he perked up to perfect posture.

"I am one of your friends," Coach redirected with his wits. "I just wanted to call to see how things were going at school, and if you were going to finish with more than eligible grades."

Ward paused for a second and then stuttered, "Yyyyyyeah thhhhhhings are going good."

Then, Coach regained the conversation, "Ward, we think that you are a great running back, but you could even be better. Grades aren't the most important part of school, but I want you to understand it is the mindset that no matter what you are doing, you are trying your hardest. That is what's important.

We need you to always play your best card, and be smart off the field as well as on the field.

We think you have a ton of potential, and once you start using all of it, great things will happen. For now, we wanted to let you know we are going to red-shirt you, and give you another year to grow into yourself." Players have an opportunity to take one redshirt year when they are on the team but are ineligible to play. This time gives them an extra year where they still practice and train but cannot compete on Saturdays.

Ward agreed with him and briefly finished the conversation, acting like he understood. He hung up the phone and muttered, "Other people keep holding me back." In his mind, other people just didn't understand his vision. All he wanted to do was play football. He knew nothing of responsibility or, more specifically, self-control.

This mindset continued to constrain him, and it wasn't until four years into his Carroll College career that he made a dramatic change. As time passed by, Ward was only the third string running back, and he even missed a season because he lost eligibility when he received two failing grades in one semester. Finally, in the spring of his junior year, Ward had a great spring game and after the scrimmage, he met Ace.

A 42-year-old beat up ex-Saint, Mason Hauser, rightfully earned the name 'Ace' in his playing days when he was the utility player for the Saints. The ace-in-the-hole was a three time All-American tight end as well as the punter, kicker and backup quarterback. He knew how to be successful in the game as well as anyone, but, more importantly, he knew how to sculpt a successful player. Ace helped coach at Carroll for many years, and he complemented Van Nest perfectly, forming a duo much like Batman and Robin. Though he didn't coach anymore, Ace never missed a Carroll scrimmage, and he still helped out from time to time.

After the scrimmage, Ace congratulated Ward and took the young man aside the field. "Ward, how many yards did you have? You must have had two-twenty or something? I can't wait to see you perform next season."

Negatively, Ward replied, "Yeah but that's how my spring went last year too. Then the season didn't amount to anything."

"Hmm." Ace suggested, "Last year was different. Last year, you weren't playing with a full deck. You were missing key aspects just like playing without aces."

Ward's negativity persisted, and he stated, "Clever words coming from someone who had so much natural talent. It's easy to criticize when you were the ace-in-the-hole."

Subsequently, Mr. Hauser elaborated, "You see, Ward, I didn't get my name because I was the 'ace-in-the-hole'. I became the 'ace-in-the-hole' because I refused to give anything except my best at everything I did. No matter what I did, I always asked myself if this were my high card, or if I were relying on winning with a lower number. I know you have aces in your deck, and I want to help you reveal them. Meet me in coach's office at three o'clock tomorrow. I have something that will help you."

Chapter 2

THE DAY THAT TURNED HIS LIFE AROUND

"You cannot change your destination overnight, but you can change your direction overnight." Jim Rohn

Very reluctant to show up, Ward managed to swallow his pride and to make an appearance the next day. Mason was sitting in coach's desk with a big smile on his face when Ward walked in. "How's your day going? Are you sore from yesterday at all?"

Instead of answering the question, Ward asked, "What's this you are going to show me?"

Ace reached into a beat-up manila envelope. "You don't like to beat around the bush, do you?" He then set a piece of paper on the desk. "This changed my life years ago, and I have no doubt it will change yours too."

GOALOGRAM

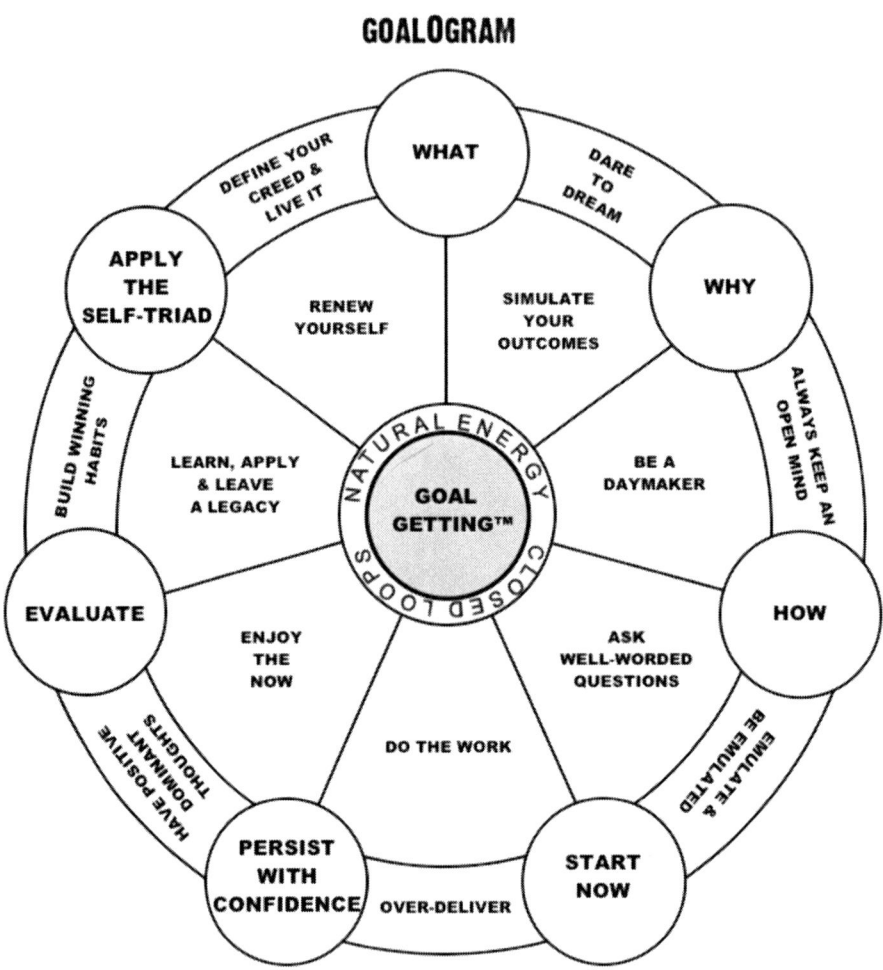

"So, how exactly is this going to help? What does all this mean? Is this like one of those tarot card things? Cuz, I don't believe in all that."

Ace confidently stated, "This is a philosophy and a proven system that helps people accomplish their goals. I call it *The Seven Essential Loops to Goal Getting* and I want to help you develop your goals for the season."

Ward said, "Yeah, I know that stuff is important. I got goals."

Without any hesitation Ace asked, "What exactly are your goals?" Ward then paused for a moment. "Uh, I want to have a great year and help my team win the championship."

Shaking his head Ace said, "That is not a goal. I don't want to seem rude, but you just made that up on the spot and it is far too vague."

"Well I meant..." Ward tried to defend himself before he was cut short by Ace again.

"Look, if I am going to continue, you are going to have to stop thinking that you know everything and let me help. Let me know when you are ready to leave your ego at the door and be a man."

Despite his constant arguments, Ward actually had great respect for Ace. This moment was one of the few times in his history where Ward felt apologetic, "I am sorry, Ace, and I'll be more polite." With a sigh of relief, Ace started the teachings.

"Take a look at the diagram. There are seven circles called 'loops', and they must be closed before you can accomplish each of your goals. We are going to focus on those seven essential loops. Completing a task is referred to as closing the 'loop', do you understand?" Ward nodded his head. "Good. Take a look at the first loop."

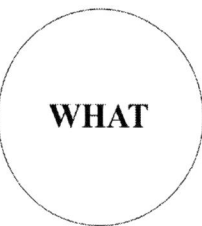

Two steps to closing the loop:
1.   What do you deeply wish to accomplish?
2.   What are the fine details of your endeavors?

Ace tossed Ward a pen and said, "I want you to answer these questions."

Without any thought Ward responded, "That's easy; I want to have good season next year."

A sour look crossed Ace's face. "That is not a goal, and that is exactly why you haven't accomplished anything since you have played here. When you write a goal, it needs to be concise and vivid, so detailed that you can close your eyes and see yourself accomplishing it." Ward eased his mind and began to answer the questions with an unusual amount of

concentration.

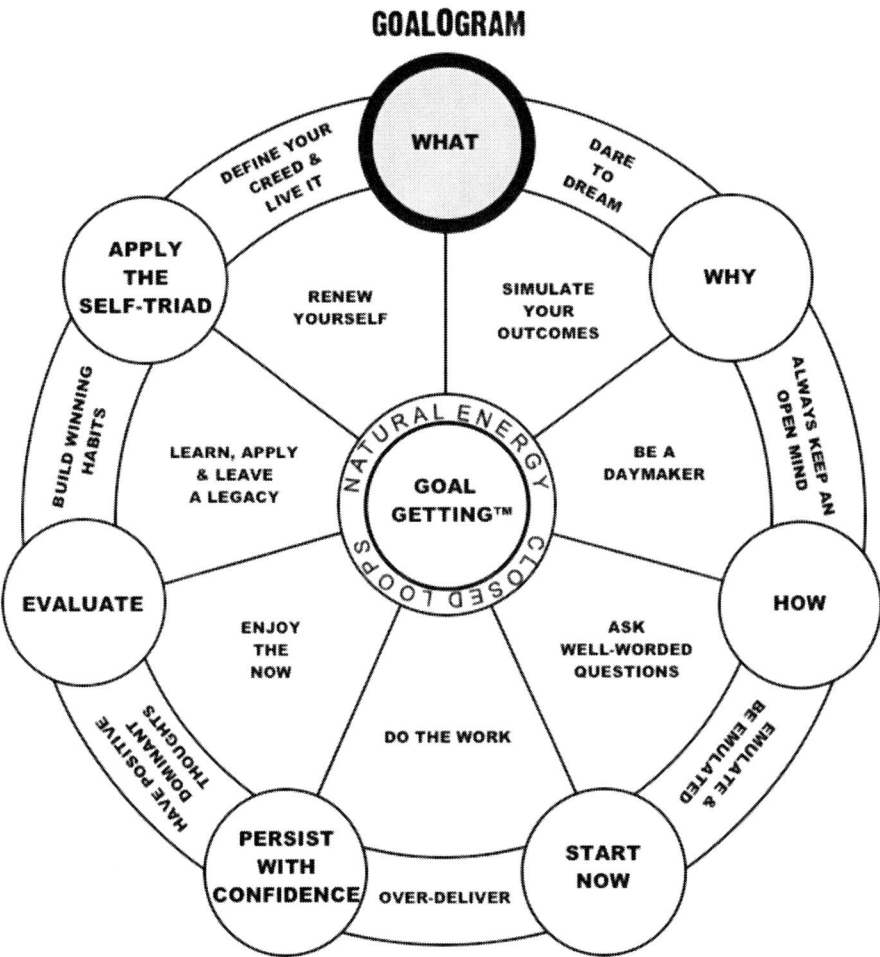

WHAT

What do you deeply wish to accomplish?

I want to be a leader on the team.

I want to be a good teammate.

I want to be the guy my opponents have to scheme for.

I want to start and finish every game in my free.

I want to put my team in the position to win.

What are the fine details to your endeavors?

I want to average over 100 yards/game.

I want to have a 3.6 G.P.A.

I want to motivate a teammate to change his lifestyle on and off the field.

I want to make all conference as an individual but be one person on a championship team.

 Before reading on, have some fun and write down a few of your goals in the space below. You can also download a FREE goalOgram at loops4biz.com/templates.php.

LOOPS 4 *YOUR* LIFE

Chapter 3

A DEEPER MEANING TO LIFE

"Happiness cannot be traveled to, owned, earned, worn or consumed. Happiness is the spiritual experience of living every minute with love, grace and gratitude." Denis Waitley

"Now we are making progress. I am very impressed that you chose to put school as your goal also. This next loop is very important. Do you know why most people don't follow through with their New Year's resolutions, Ward? Because they don't have any emotion attached to the goal. Most of the time, the person is making a generic resolution because they believe that society wants them to do so. Their friends say that they are going to lose weight so they make the same promise to themselves. The next thing they know, they fall off of the wagon on January 2nd because that particular goal has no emotional attachment to them. For that reason, you must ask, 'why', and find the key that turns your personal engine."

Perplexed momentarily, Ward simply sat. "I don't exactly understand what you want me to do. I just want to do these things to make me happy."

Ready for such a misunderstanding, Ace was prepared to respond. "I thought you would say that and let me first say that happiness cannot be contingent upon any external factors. You make your own happiness, and you don't need a goal to be happy. You need a goal to be complete. Goals give direction but not happiness. You need to be happy with yourself while you are acting on your goal, and the outcome will give you a deeper meaning. You can learn to be happy with any performance in life, but when you start accomplishing goals, you will find gratitude, the strongest human emotion. Constantly give thanks. It is equally important to give thanks to yourself, and the best way to do so is by completion of a goal."

As a sense of clarity engulfed Ward's face, his pen began to take over. Ace perked up in amazement when he saw the rate at which Ward was maturing on this project. "I thought you would come around, but you have impressed me already, Ward."

Matching Ace's posture, Ward replied, "I think this responsibility was inside me the whole time, but it feels so good to have revealed it."

GOALOGRAM

WHY

Why is this goal important to you? (family, beliefs, etcetera)

Family is what I am most passionate about and the only thing I can compare similar feelings to is football. The last 4 years have been a dark time in my life, but football is what gave me hope. When all doors were closed, football opened one and gave me a path to follow. I now see that the direction I was headed in was a dead-end. I owe this game the very best of me and I'll give just that.

Using descriptive words, write a paragraph portraying how great you will feel when you accomplish this task.

I visualize myself sitting in the gym on graduation day. Feeling grateful for having followed through with my goal and for turning my life around, I can see my family and the proud looks on their faces. Their looks send waves of honor and love into me as I accept my diploma and know that I gave it my very best.

Give Why a try! Now is the time for you to dig down and determine precisely why you desire your goals.

LOOPS 4 *YOUR* LIFE

Chapter 4

BLOOD, SWEAT, & TEARS

"Do what you say you are going to do, when you say you are going to do it, and do it that way every time."
Coach Mike Van Diest

"You've really come a long way, Ward, but remember all of this is useless unless you transfer the 'why' in your heart into the 'how'. Think of the 'how' as the *blood*, *sweat*, and *tears*."

Ward looked at Ace quizzically. "Okay. What does that mean?"

"The *blood* in the body symbolizes the connection from the heart into the hands, and the hands become the instruments for *sweat* and hard work. Finally, the *tears* represent the emotional commitment necessary to achieve your goals." Prepared for Ward's confused look, Ace smiled and continued.

"Just as your *blood* symbolizes the connection from heart to hands, so does the 'why' need a connection to the 'how'. You can have the greatest desires in the world, but if you never form a plan of action to accomplish those desires, you'll never have the vital lifeblood necessary to be successful."

Slowly, Ward started nodding as he wrapped his mind around that thought. "So *blood* symbolizes the plan of action?"

"Exactly!" exclaimed Ace.

"Nothing worth having is ever easy to get. Once you have a plan of action, you must determine how much time and effort (and how often) you are willing to commit toward achieving your goal? In other words, how much *sweat* and hard work will you commit? Be specific here. Just saying *a lot* doesn't do much good!"

"And, finally, there's no such thing as something for nothing. What are you willing to give up to accomplish your goals? If you're not willing to commit all of your *tears* (your emotional energies) to capturing your goals, then you might as well not waste your time or other's time." Ace paused and took a drink of water before finishing, "By combining all three parts: *blood*, *sweat*, and *tears*, you have all the necessary ingredients to transfer the 'why' into the 'how'.

Feeling a wave of energy overtake him as he realized the significance of this formula, Ward readied his pen and grabbed the next Loop.

GOALOGRAM

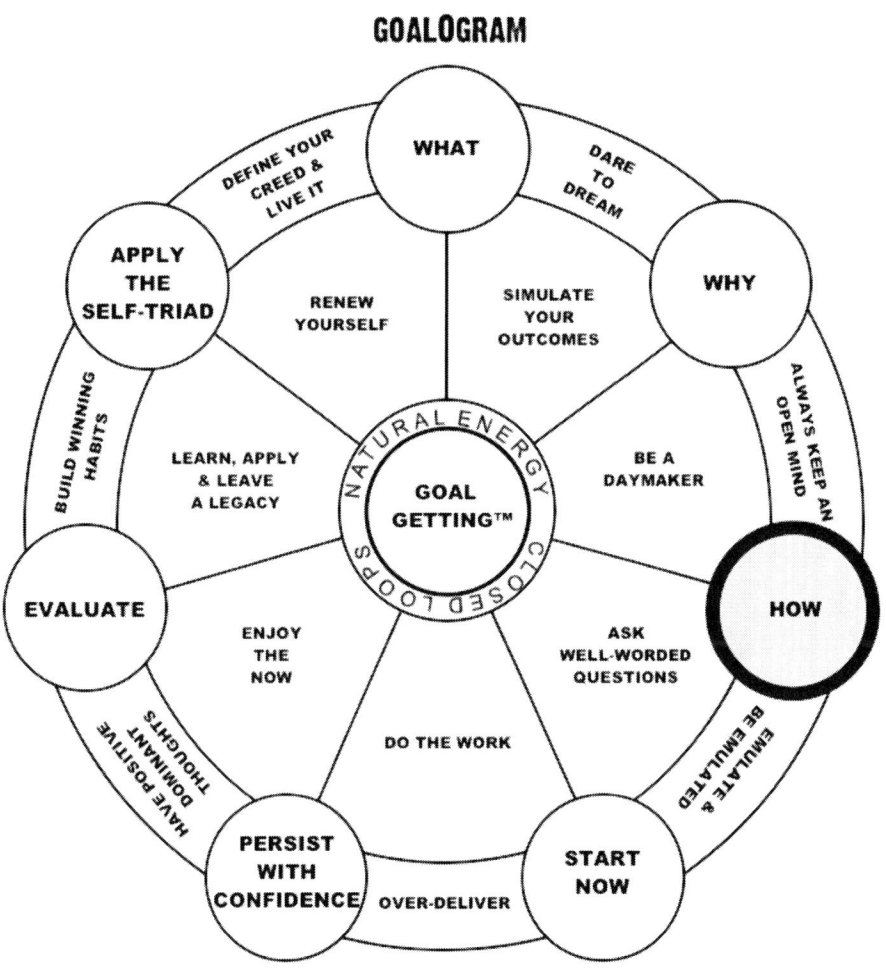

HOW

BLOOD: What actions will you take to progress towards your goal?

I will train 3 days/wk and watch film after each session
I will take Business Law in the summer so I can graduate in
the fall.
I will invite and encourage younger players to join my
workouts and film study.
I will play each play as my last and never forget this day

SWEAT: How much time and effort (and how often) will you commit to achieve your goal (Daily, Weekly, Monthly)?

I am going to give 100% and every day I will read and recite
this goal. I will always be present in meetings and practice,
every play, every practice, every week, all season long.

TEARS: What will you give up in order to reach your goal (activities, energy, focus)? No partying, and I will get 8 hours of
sleep each night. I will also give up all negative
thoughts and replace them w/ positive thoughts.

 Start your How now! In a few short sentences: 1. Start your plan. 2. Make a vow on your effort and put a date on your goal. 3. Sacrifice any poor habits that stand in your way.

LOOPS 4 *YOUR* LIFE

Chapter 5

TODAY IS THE DAY TO START

"A journey of a thousand miles begins with a single step." Lao Tzu

Seeing Ward's responses, Ace began to think he was enjoying this conversation even more than Ward! He tried to hide his excitement because he knew the next Loop (the transition from planning into doing) is often the downfall of even the best plans.

"Ward, we have gone a long ways already, but believe it or not, it's all for nothing unless you take action and Start Now."

Though he was becoming increasingly receptive to Ace's profound statements, Ward still had his doubts. "What do you mean Start Now? I thought we started over an hour ago!"

"In one sense, we have. In another sense, we haven't." Ace's cryptic sayings were starting to give Ward a sense that he was in a sequel to *The Karate Kid*.

"Okay, Mr. Miyagi, please tell me more."

"Ha!" Ace laughed. "It's great to dream; in fact, not enough people dream, but the more common problem is they don't ever take action. People like to dream big and talk big. Then they go to bed, and forget about their dreams. Later they wake up and wonder why their dreams haven't came true!"

"Okay, okay, I see what you're saying. The road to hell is paved with good intentions. We need to actually work towards our dreams if they're going to come true. Am I right?" Ward asked.

"There we go, Ward! But there's more to the thought than just that." He paused, forcing Ward to think deeper before continuing, "The real key is to Start Now. This instant. What is one action you can take right now to move closer to your goal?"

Ward racked his brain, "Right now? I can't think of anything right now."

Ace fired, "Are you going to work out tomorrow?"

"Yes," Ward replied. "What time?"

"Eight A.M."

Ace then asked, "With whom?"

"Well, Gill is supposed to show up, but I never really know with him."

"Hmm." Ace said with an intrigued tone. "Isn't one of your goals to be a leader and motivate your teammates? Why don't you call up Gill right now, and make sure he's coming tomorrow. *Close that Loop* right now."

GOALOGRAM

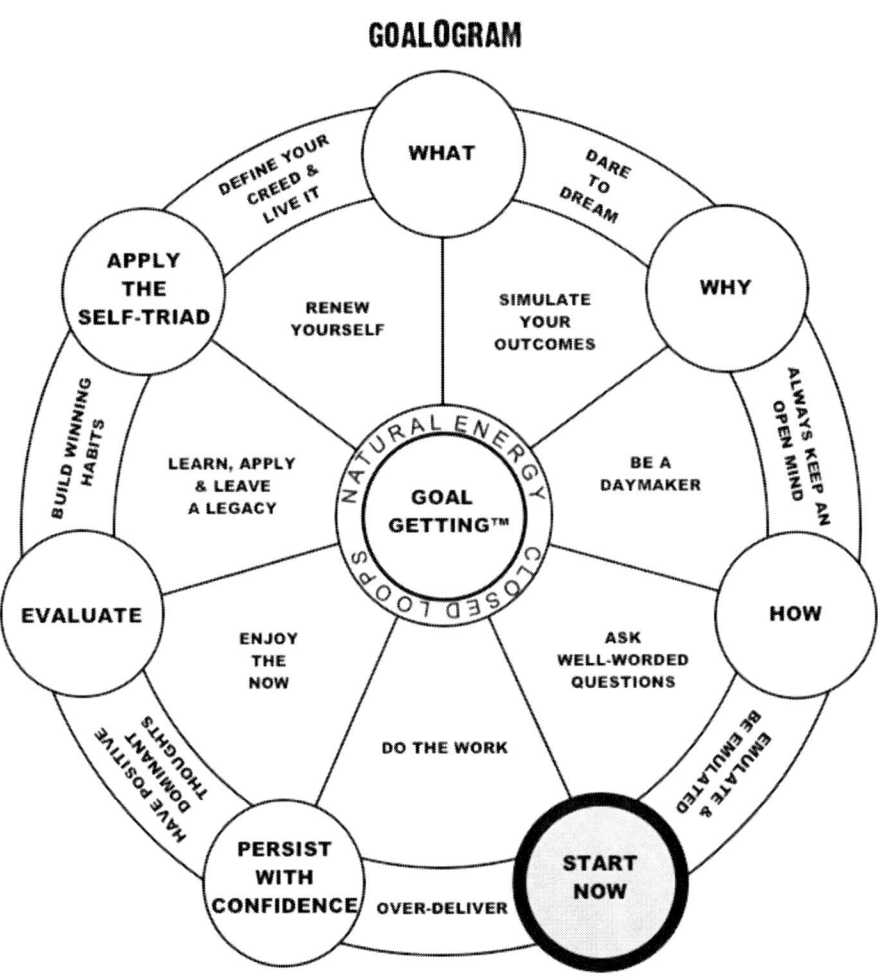

START NOW

What is one action you will you do, right NOW, this hour, and before the day is over to create momentum towards your goal?

Right now, I have called Bill and made sure he'll be at the workout tomorrow morning.

This hour, I will go to lunch and talk about my goals for next season with my friends.

Before the day is over, I will do my homework before any distractions hold me back.

How can you continually make sure that you will always act NOW?

I will always take action on my ideas or goals immediately, and never "sleep on it."

I will accomplish this by always telling myself to "Close the loop" with every thought that I have, and also at the end of every practice, workout, and meeting.

 "It's now or never! I ain't gonna live forever!" – Bon Jovi

LOOPS 4 *YOUR* LIFE

After a few minutes of overcoming his teammate's excuses, Ward confirmed that his lifting partner would be there tomorrow morning. Ward smiled, "Hey, that feels pretty good. I believe I'm already getting the ball rolling."

"Exactly! That's why it's vital to *Start Now*. You now have created momentum so that your little snowflake can turn into a snowball which will soon transform into an avalanche!"

Ward was feeling on fire, "I am really excited, Ace! Thanks for your help. This conversation has been great!"

"That's wonderful to hear, Ward. Now you will be able to start a powerful ball of momentum. The next step is one that..."

Ward cut him off. "I think this is what I have been missing. I do appreciate your help, but I have to run." The meeting was going into the second hour, and Ward wanted to make lunch with his friends.

"But there are still more essential Loops we need to go over." Ace attempted to keep his student, but Ward was adamant.

"I am really thankful, Ace. I know this is what I've been missing, but now I'm ready to make things happen!"

When he finished his sentence, he stood, reached out his hand which Ace shook as he softly replied, "Glad I could help." He continued to hold the handshake as he said, "Don't hesitate to call me if you want to talk any further." Then as Ward ran off to meet his friends in the cafeteria, he nodded his head in confirmation.

Chapter 6

A TURN FOR THE WORSE

"You cannot plan the most important events in your life – they happen to you." Rob Riemen

After taking the first real concrete steps towards his goals, Ward wanted to take several more as soon as possible. As the final weeks of the semester came to a close, he felt on a roll and couldn't wait for the season to begin. In addition to being in the same lifting group, Gill and Ward were developing a close friendship. Even better, Ward was seeing his enthusiasm rub off on many of his fellow teammates. It seemed everyday brought him closer to his goals.

However, when semester finals came, Ward was less than prepared. He devoted so much time and energy on the fun and easy part of his goal, studying had taken a back seat. He didn't find World History as captivating as building a stronger team. Furthermore, Ward's grade took a turn for the worse the day each student had to present a speech on 'freedom.' The girl presenting before Ward, Albina, a foreign exchange student from Kyrgyzstan, told a personal story of traditional arranged marriages in Kyrgyzstan. After gaining permission from a daughter's father, the male suitor would perform the tradition of 'Bride Kidnapping,' where he would forcefully kidnap the woman and make her his wife. One day, Albina's sister told her of the conversation she overheard between their father and a male suitor concerning Albina; she was going to be kidnapped! With the help of her closest friends, Albina escaped to America. She finished her speech noting how grateful she was for a culture that protects an individual's freedom.

When it was Ward's turn, he rose, slowly walked to the front of class thinking, "That's a tough act to follow." For the next five minutes Ward told of William Wallace, with his only reference the movie 'Braveheart.' As he was giving the speech, he realized just how unprepared he felt. Struggling with his speech, he was unable to stop saying "uh" and "ah" in between each sentence. He finished his speech by saying how shameful it was that Wallace fought so hard for freedom, but died before he could experience it. Once everyone had spoken, Ward was the first from the classroom thankful he was done with the class.

With grades slipping and summer in the near future, Ward found it hard to stay focused on both school and football. He was excited that so many players were staying in Helena for the whole summer. On Monday, the weight room was packed and Ward could hear the clanking of metal plates. He hurried his pace to join his teammates, but ran into Coach Hogan. "What's up, Hoges?"

"You are." Coach Hogan responded. "But actually, Ward, Coach would like to see you in his office, now." Uneasily Ward started towards the football offices.

Taking those final steps to Coach Van Nest's half-open door, Ward took a deep breath and timidly knocked on the door. "Come in, Ward." Coach Van Nest said in a straightforward voice. "Have a seat."

To say Coach Mike Van Nest was an intimidating person would be an understatement. Having won five National Championships in six years will do that. Even more than the championships, Van Nest's high standards for his players went far beyond the field. He expected these young college students to strive for perfection in all that they did, whether on the field, in the classroom, or in their relationships with family and friends. In short, he expected them to become men. This standard of integrity was summarized in his favorite saying, "*Do what you say you are going to do, when you say you are going to do it, and do it that way every time.*"

After a moment of silence, Ward asked, "What's on your mind, Coach?"

"Ward, you've come a long way since you were a freshman. A team is only as good as the seniors who lead it, and I have been happy to see you become one of those leaders this spring."

"Thanks, Coach. It seems like ages ago when all the freshmen had to do bear crawls because I kept wearing my hat in the classroom!" Ward smiled.

"That brings me to why I called you in here, Ward." Coach took over the conversation. "I have been notified that you failed

World History. Since this failure lowers our team's GPA, we have less scholarship money and one less player will be able to be on the active roster next fall." Ward's heart sank deep into his stomach. "Not only does that make me not trust you, Ward, but it also means that you have lost your eligibility for the upcoming season."

As Coach allowed his words to sink in, Ward felt like the ground beneath him had crumbled. All his hard work and energy from this spring and all the years previous seemed to have suddenly become worthless. Coach proceeded to talk about summer school and regaining eligibility with summer classes, but his words fell on deaf ears. Using all his energy not to cry in front of coach, Ward could only think how he had let down his teammates, his family, and himself. Excused from Coach's office, he immediately left the PE Center in his car.

Driving around the outskirts of town for what seemed like an eternity but was really only a few hours, Ward couldn't stop repeating to himself, "Why did this have to happen to me?" In a climax of emotions, Ward parked the car on a dirt road and started pitching out all of his football gear and notes into the ditch. As he dumped out the last binder, it hit the ground and out popped a single piece of paper, the uncompleted *goalOgram.*

Staring at the sheet of paper that had almost magically appeared before him, Ward felt some new feeling come over him. A feeling of hope.

Chapter 7

WHEN THE STUDENT IS READY

"Persisting in your path, though you forfeit the little, you gain the great." Ralph Waldo Emerson

The next day, Ace was waiting in Coach Van Nest's office. Coach knew Ward would return and he asked Ace to consult the young man. Entering the same office he had left less than twenty-four hours ago gave Ward an eerie feeling. Ace had Coach's chair rolled over to the TV as he played with the DVD player, blowing in it like it was an original Nintendo console. Ace heard him approaching, "Take a seat Ward."

Surprised to see Ace, Ward waited for him to turn around as the older man calmly said over his shoulder, "You ever hear of Sylvester Stallone?" Ace continued before Ward could utter a sound. "Many people make fun of Sly because of his voice, never giving him credit for his genuine acting. Not many people know when he was born, the doctors had to use forceps that severed a nerve causing paralysis in part of his face. For this reason, he permanently has a slurred speech. No one seems to get past that slur." Rather softly, Ace added, "But if you watch Sly and listen to him, you'll see how real his performance is, and how true his pain is."

"I guess I've never gotten past that myself," Ward said reflectively.

With his back still turned and playing with the remote, Ace

replied, "The only thing greater than the story of 'Rocky' is the story of Stallone. Did you know that Stallone wrote the script for 'Rocky'? His dream was to act as the main character. At the time he was a no-name actor with a speech problem, but he continually filled his mind with positive, dominant thoughts. One of the movie studios thought he had a good script, and wanted to buy the rights to his script without him playing Rocky Balboa. Though he badly needed the money, Stallone refused the offer because he was convinced he had to play Rocky. The studio offered more and more money, but he continued to say 'no.' In the process, he lost his girlfriend and even his best friend, his dog."

Spinning in his chair, Ace stared Ward straight in the eyes, "Through all the turmoil, Stallone persisted because he had self-confidence. Eventually, the studio agreed to Stallone's terms and the rest is history." Ace finished his story.

Ward paused before responding, "I don't see how all this Stallone material applies to me. I failed World History, and now I have to take two summer classes on top of summer workouts, *and* on top of my full-time summer construction job. How am I supposed to handle all that?"

"Start by getting a better attitude!" Ace snapped back.

Feeling a little offended as Ace stared at him, Ward began to reply when Ace hit the play button and an older Rocky Balboa filled the TV screen:

Let me tell you something you already know... [Life] is about how hard you can get hit and keep moving forward. How much you can take and keep moving forward. That's how winning is done! Now if you know what you're worth, then go out and get what you're worth. But ya gotta be willing to take the hits.

The screen went blank. A short silence filled the room before Ward stood up and said, "I can take the hits, Ace! I've been in that weight room three days a week and..."

"Not those kind of hits!" Ace cut him off powerfully. "The physical challenges are the easy parts, but the real question is. Can you take what *life* hits you with? Can you keep moving forward everyday, even on those days when you don't feel like it? Anyone can confidently move forward when they've got the wind at their back, but what about when the wind is against them? Do they shell up, or do they push through confidently ahead staring directly at the goal in front of them? When the wind stops blowing or changes direction, you have to paddle harder."

Ward had never heard Ace raise his voice before, and this intensity commanded his full attention. At that moment, he saw his training buddy Gill walk by. Probably checking to see what was taking him so long. They were supposed to start training 15 minutes ago. Hearing the severity of the conversation, Gill tiptoed away realizing he would be on his own for the day.

Ace continued, "Too many people waste too much time fretting over whether they are making the right or wrong decision. Let me tell you something. The only wrong decision is the one made half-heartedly. A decision isn't "right" when it is made. It is made, then it is *made* right!"

Lowering his voice a notch, Ace said, "When you *persist with confidence*, every day you move closer to your goal, no matter how small the step, how inglorious the task, or how difficult the action. You keep moving forward because you believe in yourself. That's what separates the ordinary from the extraordinary."

Again Ward was silent, but this time he understood. Ace slid the next piece of paper in front of him. "This should have been filled out a long time ago. I tried to explain all of the loops must be closed for you to accomplish your task. Nevertheless, it is not too late."

For a brief moment Ward felt ashamed of his immaturity. He wondered, "Is this what growing up is about?"

However, this shame soon left as his newfound understanding encouraged him to start writing.

GOALOGRAM

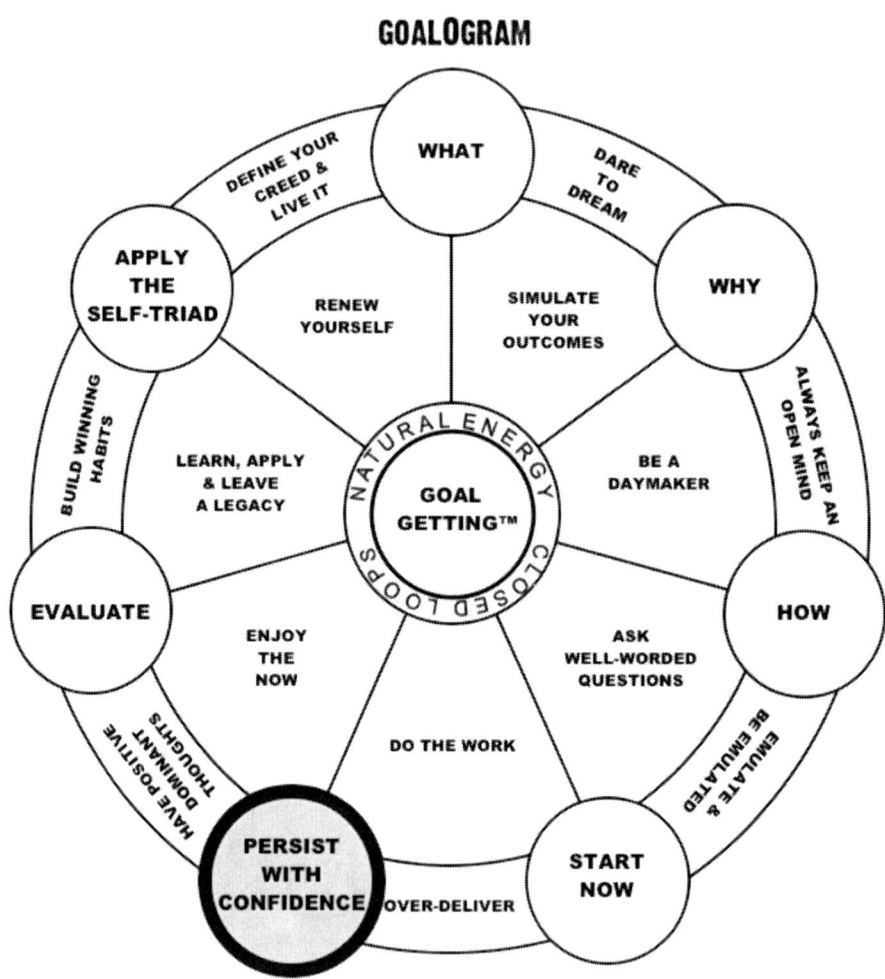

PERSIST WITH CONFIDENCE

How will you handle what Life "hits" you with and keep moving forward?

When the going gets tough, I will re-read the WIN Loop and re-focus on how great I'll feel when I achieve my goal.

How will you *make* your decisions the "right" decisions?

I will never hesitate in my thoughts or in my actions, because I believe in my teammates, my coaches, and myself. Because of this, I will follow through with total confidence in my decisions.

 Take some 'hits' and Keep Moving Forward. Brick walls will stand in your way. Predict any obstacles and write how you will overcome them.

LOOPS 4 *YOUR* LIFE

Chapter 8

CHECK YOUR PROGRESS

"Even though you are on the right track, you will get run over if you just sit there." Will Rogers

"This next lesson comes with perfect timing." Ward perked up, and listened. "Sometimes we get off track, Ward, and doing so isn't the big deal. The big deal is that you get back on the right track as soon as possible. Did you know that when a torpedo is flying through the air locked on target, it sometimes veers off the straight path? However, the torpedo has a built-in negative feedback mechanism that warns when it veers, and it then realigns itself."

"Do you think coach is still mad at me for flunking my test?" Ward asked.

"Well, we can either sit here and worry, or we can jump back on the path. What do you think is the most productive?" Ward nodded his head in consent. "You see, Ward, it is not a good thing to flunk a test or fail anything, but it is far worse to bathe in self-pity. For one reason or another, we miss the target, but that is not a bad thing. Failure is not the end result of missing the target; experience is. We all must remember to look at failures as increasing your odds as opposed to resenting previous behaviors. Every failure puts you one step closer to success. Also, I want you to eliminate worry, self-pity and resentment from your life entirely and develop your own negative feedback mechanism to monitor your progress."

Ward knew what to do next, and he grabbed the paper and started writing.

GOALOGRAM

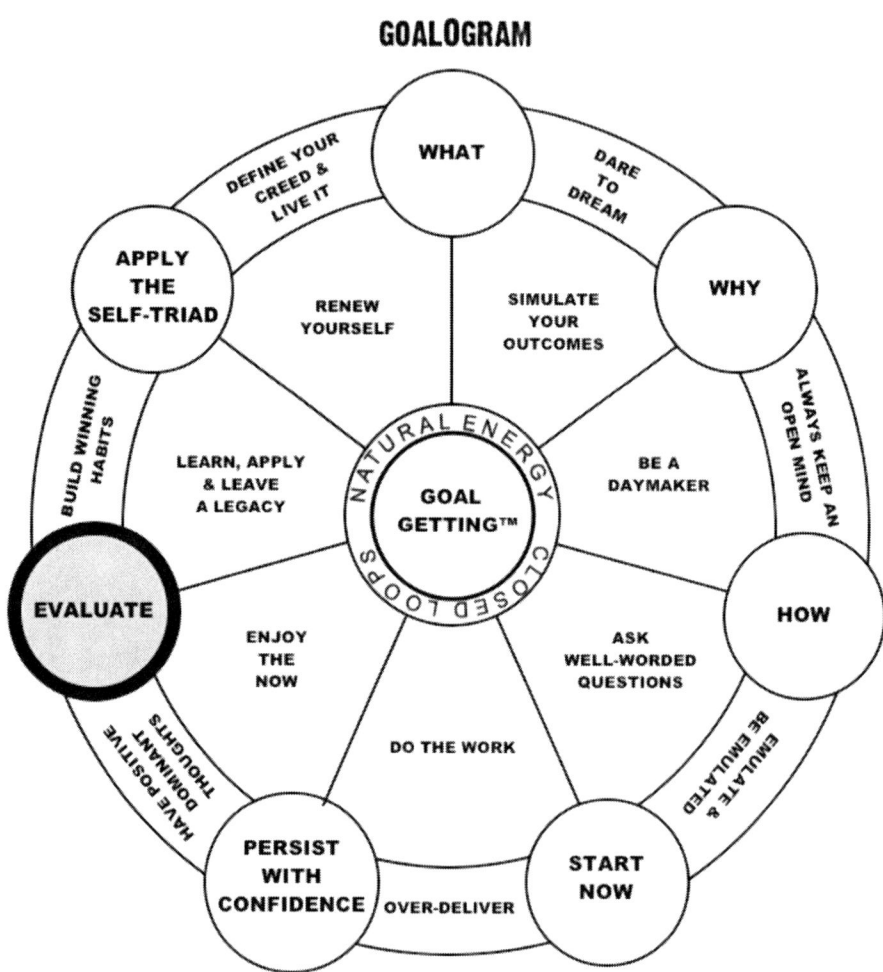

EVALUATE

How will you monitor your progress?

I will evaluate myself by my numbers on the field, in the weight room, and my knowledge of our offense.

As film and practice progress, I expect to get better every day.

I will write in a journal nightly in reference to my goals.

How often will you monitor your progress?

Every day I will ask myself if I am doing everything I can do to improve.

Every week I will ask Coach if I am doing everything I can do to improve.

Every week I will recap my journal entries.

Every month I will meet with him.

Set up your own grading system. Every day, we like to recollect on our efficiency and see where we can improve. Large goals are evaluated weekly, on Sunday evenings.

LOOPS 4 *YOUR* LIFE

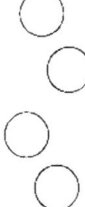

Chapter 9

SCULPT YOUR CHARACTER

"Work harder on yourself than you do on your job." Jim Rohn

"Before I finish this last loop, can I run into the gym to tell Gill that I am not going to make it today? I promise I will be right back."

Ace nodded, "I'm sure he figured that out an hour ago but go ahead."

Ward ran out of coach's office and into the gym where Gill was helping a few freshmen kids with their sprinting form. Gill paused and yelled, "Hey, Ward, watch these guys' form; I think they are really starting to get it."

Nodding in agreement Ward said, "Yeah, that's way better this week. Hey, sorry I missed today; I'm just working on some stuff with Ace."

While everyone kept doing what they were doing, one of the freshmen, gasping for air, answered with a sarcastic tone. "That's alright; we think Gill is a better teacher anyway."

Ward smirked back as he reversed his sprint toward coach's office and yelled, "Don't get used to that 'softy'; I'll be back tomorrow."

Ace was observing from the corner of the gym, and Ward shifted to a lower gear, surprised to see him watching. "You know, Ward, Coach Van Nest wanted me to complement you on helping motivate Gill. Apparently, he saw Gill walking around with his *goalOgram, and* the credit went back to you. It is very mature not only to work on your life, but to also help mentor others. Coach said that Gill must not have been the only player you helped because the results of captain's vote are in, and he wanted me to tell you personally that the players voted you to be a captain."

Ward's face looked like he just walked into the wrong bathroom. "Are you serious? Man, that's one of my goals. They're coming true already."

A sparkle shined from Ace's eye. "You are truly a leader. Coach has scheduled a players' meeting where you will lead the players in defining the team's goals before the season. First, we had better close the last loop on your *goalOgram.* Follow me."

As he led Ward outside, Ace grabbed his jacket. "Let's take a walk, and I can tell you about the next lesson." Ward pulled his hood over his head to fend off the brisk breeze. "You are now aware times aren't always going to be easy, and there will be brick walls standing in your way. This plateau is inevitable, and before you hit another brick wall, you need to fully adopt and apply the self-triad."

Ward gave a bewildered stare, "You had better explain that one because it sounds more weird than when you told me about the *blood, sweat* and *tears.*" Ace nodded in agreement. "Think of this triad as the characteristics you need to carry out the blood, sweat and tears, and as a compilation of three characteristics all successful people have in common. The first of the triad is self-control. I know that you have heard this thought before, but in simple terms, self-control equals responsibility. When things don't go your way, you cannot blame other people. No matter what the outcome, you have to adopt the philosophy 'if it is meant to be, it is up to me.' Too often in life, people are quick to point the finger at everyone but themselves."

As they approached the stadium gate, Ace reached in his pocket and pulled out a rusty key. They opened the gate and nonchalantly walked past the 'Under Maintenance' sign onto the field. "Ten years ago, a Carroll player showcased the perfect example of self-control. We were playing Tech, and they were kicking our butts. Senior cornerback Marcus Miller was having an average game, and he could have kept playing average with no fault for the loss. Miller had a different idea though." Ace grew emotional, engaging himself in the story. "Marcus adopted the mentality 'if it is meant to be, it is up to me.' I will never forget what it felt like the day he returned two interceptions for touchdowns. We were tied 14-14, and on our last drive, we were stopped on the thirty when Marcus proceeded to kick the game winning field goal. The smallest player on our team scored all 17 points and won the game for us."

With a huge smile, Ward spoke up, "I have heard about that game. Coach tells us every year before fall camp starts."

"Yes, it is a great story, and it has become somewhat of a tradition to tell. There is another lesson that can be learned from that story, and it is the second of the self-triad. Self-discipline is basically the opposite of giving up. We should be excited when we hit a brick wall because that means now there is something to accomplish. If there weren't a wall, there wouldn't be anything to accomplish. You see, if I gave you a ball right now, would you call it a touchdown if you ran across the goal line?"

"I guess not," Ward replied.

"Exactly! It isn't a touchdown until you run past the other eleven guys that are trying to stop you."

"I have never looked at it that way before."

Ace noticed Ward was beginning to shiver. "Let's walk back inside, and I'll tell you about the last of the self-triad, self-image. Self-image is the foundation of a person's well being, and other people can only see you as a fraction of how you see yourself. I always like to say that ugly people are not ugly because they are actually unattractive, but because they think they are unattractive."

The student and his mentor made their way back to the office and hunger pains overwhelmed the retired football star.

"Alright, Ward, ask me your questions now because I am going to dinner."

"I think I have it. I am going to stay here for a couple more minutes and fill out my last loop."

GOALOGRAM

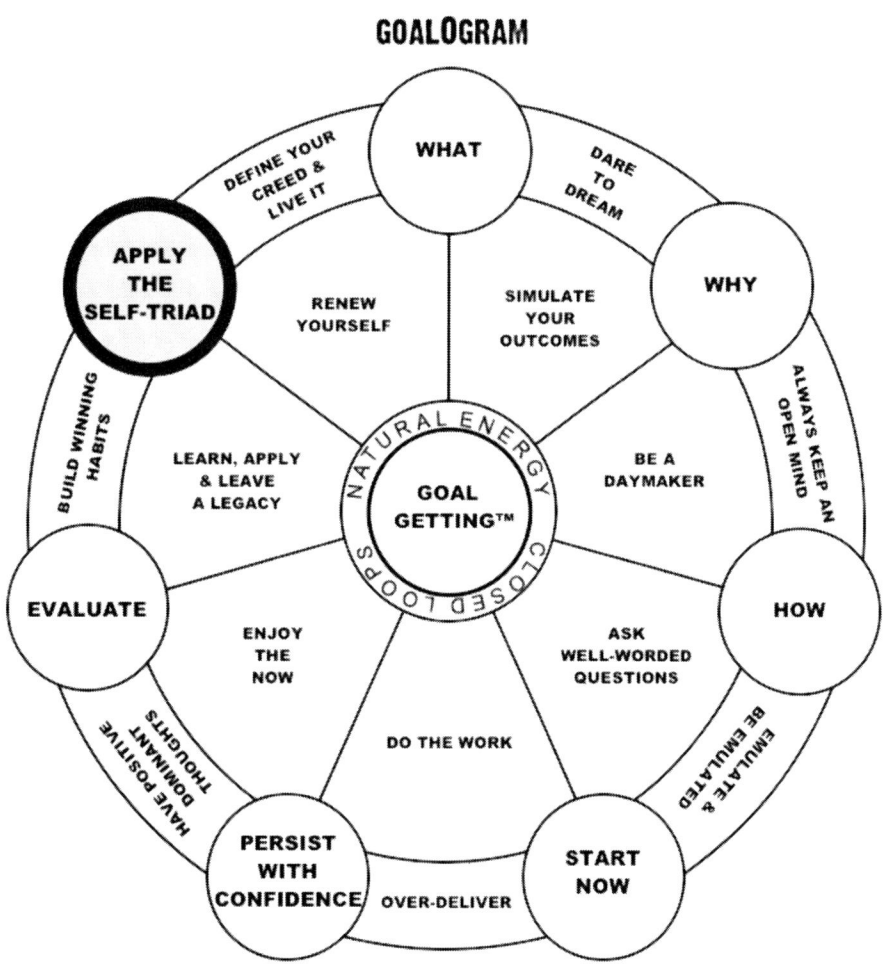

Apply the Self-Triad

Self-Control: Equals responsibility.

- Recite the phrase 'if it is meant to be, it is up to me' daily.

Self-Discipline: The opposite of giving up.

- Promise yourself to welcome challenges and never to take the easy route.

Self-Image: The foundation that supports your well-being.

-Write in all of the positive descriptive words of how your personality will be when you reach your goal. Make it a statement and act that way now.

I am an adult, and like an adult I take full responsibility for my actions. I am in control of my future and my destiny. I am a man of integrity, understanding and compassion. No matter the obstacle, I will prevail.

 Bulletproof your success! Rework the Self-Triad to define you personally. List your positive traits and promise yourself to follow through with the efforts. *The most important promises you make are the ones to yourself.*

LOOPS 4 *YOUR* LIFE

Chapter 10

DON'T SETTLE FOR ANYTHING LESS

"I challenge you to make your life a masterpiece. I challenge you to join the ranks of those people who live what they teach, who walk their talk." Anthony Robbins

As planned, summer ended and Ward passed both of his summer classes with an A and a B+. Now eligible again, his life was traveling on the proper path, and it was time to put all of his hard work to use. Finally the season was about to start, and the night before their first game, Coach brought in t-shirts for everyone with the team goal on the back. Also, Ward had met with the team and led a group focus session flushing out the season goal.

Carroll College Fighting Saint's Season Goal

"To grow together as a team, creating an unbreakable brotherhood bond that places us in a position to win every game, one game at a time, by doing what we say we are going to do, when we say we are going to do it, every time."

Just like their goal stated, they set out to win the first game of the season, and they did. Then, they won the conference by focusing on one game at a time. Just like a fairy tale, Ward helped lead the Fighting Saints to victory after victory. They won the first round of the playoffs, the quarterfinals, the semifinals, and they found themselves heading to the National Championship.

They were more prepared for this final game than any they had faced so far, but there was still a distinct sense of worry throughout the team. After meetings, the night before the big game, an emotional receiver stood up and spoke, "Look, guys. No matter what happens tomorrow, we have had a great year, and I have had a lot of fun already."

"Yeah." Another player stood up, "Second place in the nation isn't that bad either."

This mediocre attitude began to replicate, and Gill whispered to Ward. "You already have 1,500 yards this season, and you have already met your individual goals, haven't you?"

"No!" Ward stood up. "That's not who we are, and we will not settle for anything less than who we are." The worried feeling began to leave the room and comfort slowly replaced it as Ward gave one of the best speeches anyone has ever heard.

This game right here is what we train for. I have seen you all work way too hard to come here and quit. That's not football, that's not who we are. We've pushed ourselves further than we thought possible; we have trained for failure in the off-season so that failure is not an option in season. I'll be damned if we are going to sit here and give up. If we lose, let it be because they earned it. Make them earn everything they get tomorrow, no freebies. Defense, you guys are the gatekeepers of that end zone and NO ONE shall enter without deserving it. Offense, let's go out there and play smash mouth football like we have been all year. We're one step away from achieving our ultimate goal, men; we have come too far to turn away from it now. Fear is not an option! We play with pride, and we play with a swagger that forces our opponents to quit. We will not be denied our destiny, men, but it's going to take every single person in this room tomorrow. For the seniors, this is it! This is the game that is going to seal our legacy; this is the game that is going to define who we are, and we are not a team that fears anyone or quits. This is the greatest stage of them all, brothers, and we're playing a very good team, but don't you forget that we are a very good team as well. This game is about us, no one else but us. We play for each other, and you can believe that I will play myself into the ground for you guys. Our bodies are fueled by purple and gold. We are one family, with one goal and one heart. When you step on that field tomorrow, leave everything you have out there. Play relentless with a passion that cannot be unmatched, men. Play for and with your brothers, for he who sheds his blood with me shall forever be my brother.

-    *Actual Speech from Carroll Saints*

Chapter 11

VICTORY COMES IN MANY SHAPES AND SIZES

"Once you hear the details of victory, it is hard to distinguish it from defeat." Jean-Paul Sarte

The opening whistle sounded and the battle began series after series. The two teams went back and forth, and each team answered each other's every stride. The University of Souix Falls (USF) was easily the biggest and strongest team Ward had ever faced. Carroll led by one point until late in the forth quarter. When the score shifted to 32-27 when Sioux Falls scored with two minutes left on the clock. Down by five points, the Saints needed one more touchdown to walk away with a win. Quick passes to the sidelines helped conserve the clock as they closed the distance toward the goal line. One 44-yard pass left Carroll on the 1 yard-line with 5 seconds left in the National Championship. The Saints took their final timeout, and there was only enough time on the clock for one more play.

One second before the play clock ran out, Ward received the handoff and hit the hole with one final burst of hope. Stopped right at the line-of-scrimmage, he spun out of the clawing pile and made a final sprint toward the corner of the end zone. The crowd erupted when Ward ran right over the top of the defensive end leaving only one more man to beat. The 220-pound running back was one-on-one in the open field with USF's outside linebacker. They collided on the goal line like two battering rams in total sacrifice. Ward's body reacted and summoned all of the hard work his off-season training built up. Every last bit of fight reached the ball for the goal line, and the play clock hit zero, sounding the buzzer. Did the ball cross the goal line? Everyone in the stadium stood silent as they waited for the official's signal. Never before has a hand signal felt like a kick to the groin until the referee waived his arms signaling that the captain's final effort was a failure.

For a moment in Helena, Montana, time had completely stopped. Then, the cheers of the opposing team shattered the ten seconds of silence. Like a thief in the night, the new National Champions took every last bit of enthusiasm away from the men in purple. Both the fans and the players felt their emotions on the down slope of the bell-shaped curve. Parents and family members dispersed on the field to comfort their fallen soldiers, and Ward was soon surrounded by all of his friends and family. Except Ace. He could see Ace standing on the sideline with that same emotionless look seemingly unaffected by the loss. In the gloom of the day, the only sparkle from anyone wearing purple came from the blue eyes of the 42-year-old veteran. They made eye contact briefly before Ace was the first person to exit the stadium.

Chapter 12

OPTIMISM EXISTS IN EVERY FAILURE

"My imperfections and failures are as much a blessing from God as my successes and talents." Mahatma Gandhi

Monday after the game brought Ward to his knees in Coach's office. "I don't know what I'm gonna do now, Coach."

The chair spun around to reveal Ace waiting for Ward's arrival. As it had so many times before, that same wise tone stunned the negativity. "How would winning that game have solved your disorientation?"

Back to defending his feelings, Ward replied. "That game is what I have worked so hard for all of my life. Don't you understand? No! You wouldn't understand because you ended your career with a victory."

This statement gently raised Ace out of his chair and he responded with unrevealed evidence. "Do you see these scars?" Ace said as he unveiled four 5-inch incisions on his left knee. "I tore every ligament in my knee in the last series of the Superbowl when we lost to the New York Giants in 87'. I won my last college game, but went on to lose my last game ever. I was lined up in the backfield and made about two steps with the handoff before Lawrence Taylor hit me like a freight train. One year in the NFL was all I had before my career hit rock bottom."

Ward retracted his outburst with a newfound approach. "What was it like to have your life's training come to an abrupt end like that?"

Ace cleared his throat, "All things have to come to an end. However, it is not about how the journey ends, it is about what you learned from your journey. Sure you wanted to win that big and final game, so did I. But you should be proud of yourself for what you have accomplished along the way. Remember, the fruits of your labor are only a temporary pleasure unless you plant seeds for the next harvest."

Understandingly Ward said, "I see what you mean, but I just lost the National Championship. I can never go back and play it again."

"I feel for you," Ace said. "I felt the same way when I was in your shoes. However, I have found from years of recollection, those games we played are actually only individual plays in the much bigger game of life. The game of life can only end one way, and whether you win or lose is not dependent upon the trophies you have gained but the legacy you have left. Remember, the game is not over. You just got stopped on first down. Now pick yourself up, learn from your mistakes, and keep your feet moving forward."

Chapter 13

THE SECOND HALF IN THE GAME OF LIFE

"The more sand that has escaped from the hourglass of our life, the clearer we should see through it." Niccolo Machiavelli

One week later, Ward finished his last college exam and went on to graduate after the fall semester. The ex-football standout walked with a sense of pride as he wore his purple cap and gown. Previously, he had only felt this way after a victory on the football field. Graduation had been a long time coming, and Ward finally jumped through every hoop and closed every loop college put in his way. "We are very proud of you, Ward," his mother said as she kissed the graduate on the cheek.

His father reiterated, "I can't think of anyone I would rather call my son. You have matured so much in the last year."

He felt a little embarrassed in front of his fellow friends in purple gowns, but instead of running from his emotions like the old Ward, a hug and a kiss he gave in return. "I guess it is time for the next realm of life," Ward said with a sense of eagerness.

"The next realm, huh? What do you foresee happening in this next realm?" Jarrod said.

"I see it like this, Dad. Everyone always tells me that you can do and be anything that you want, but I rarely see them follow through with this idea. Most people are stuck in jobs they hate, and they can't wait to clock out and get to the weekend. I am going to have a job where I love every minute, and I won't mind working overtime because it is my passion. I want to start my own restaurant."

Ward's parents smiled as each other responded in perfect unison just as if they had rehearsed it a millions times, "I never could picture you working for anybody else, you always have to get your way just like ..." Both parents pointed at each other. They all laughed and finished with one last hug.

One month later, Ward was in a suit signing paperwork at the bank. "You are very lucky to have your dad co-sign this note," The lackluster president of the local bank explained to Ward. "Money is not easy to come by in this day and age, and it would have been a long and nearly impossible run at getting a small business loan being a young man without any assets whatsoever. As long as your dad's name is on the loan, we are not worried about a thing."

Jarrod added, "And as long as you can make the payments, I am not worried about a thing. Let's not make a habit of this, but your mom and I are here to help you get your feet under you."

Everything was perfect about this business venture. The downtown location had high foot traffic and a large percentage of the population drove by the restaurant daily. *Little Sicily* was the name, and it was, believe it or not, the only Italian restaurant in Helena. *Little Sicily* stood on 312 Fuller Street, and represented Ward's new game time stadium. Finally, the best part about the endeavor was the passionate man on a mission behind the project.

Ward had a love for Italian food, and he recruited his chef from the best culinary school in Florence, Italy. Even his sous-chef was more than capable of being the head chef at any comparable restaurant. Not only were the chef's credentials legitimate, but everyone also loved the food, and the restaurant was packed Monday through Sunday.

Ward ran the business by the book. Flood the local market with advertising, get people in the restaurant, feed them what they want, and send them out full. This plan was working for the first two years, and Ward was truly living out his dream. However, things were slowly taking a turn. For some reason the numbers were not matching up anymore. *Little Sicily* was still a local favorite, but the traffic had slowed down tremendously. Perhaps the economy was responsible for the hard times. "Yeah, the economy, no one can make a living in the restaurant industry in this day and age." Ward assured himself as he stared at the last three mortgage stubs he was unable to pay.

Chapter 14

IF IT'S MEANT TO BE, IT'S UP TO ME

"People are always blaming their circumstances for what they are. I don't believe in circumstances." George Bernard Shaw

"Why does it take you so long to build up a business, when it can fall apart in a second?" Ward asked himself this question as the realism of his failing business began to set in. In an effort to conserve expenses, Ward began to lay people off and to replace their labor with his own. Something must have been miscalculated, however, because the saved paychecks did not even come close to solving the problem. He was flying downhill in a spiral and couldn't seem to find any brakes.

Though the tunnel showed no sign of light for Ward, one day, a man walked into the restaurant and offered a solution. "He most certainly isn't from around here," a lady whispered to her husband. "Look at those shoes; you can't buy those exotic skins in Montana." A matching alligator briefcase with a gold emblem laser engraved saying 'Walt Goldman' was softly set on the table for two as the hostess seated the out-of-towner.

A nervous cocktail waitress handed Mr. Goldman a drink menu, "Can I start you off with something to drink, Sir?"

The man replied with a clear tone like that of a radio jockey, "I will have a bottle of the Dehlinger Pinot Noir, and please send Ward Young out when he gets a free moment."

Usually, the staff will send out a manager instead of bothering Ward every time someone asks, but something about this guy meant business. Before he entered the floor, Ward peaked from the kitchen. "I have no idea who this guy is," Ward thought as he approached the well-dressed man.

"Ah, Mr. Young, a pleasure to meet you. I am Walt Goldman," he said before he began to pour Ward a glass of pinot. "I assume you drink wine. Or do you still have those college tendencies for cheap beer?" Somewhat insulted, a sour look took over Ward's face. "I do not mean any disrespect. I just like to poke a little fun at our younger entrepreneurs. I am here to make you an offer." As he listened attentively, the sour look began to wash away from the twenty-six-year-old's face. The alligator briefcase unlatched itself on the table and a folder titled 'Little Sicily' emerged. "My friends at the bank say that you aren't fairing so well, and I will offer you a solution. I'm a busy man so I'll get right to the point. My home is Chicago, but I have recently bought a summer cabin in Montana so I can enjoy the fishing months. To get the most bang out of my buck, and time, I decided to look into what the restaurant business was like in Helena. As I can see, it's no Chicago." That sour look crept back on Ward's face. Before he could talk, Goldman ended the conversation. "I don't know exactly how much you are behind, but I would like to buy the building and the business." He took his last drink of wine, stood up and handed

Ward the offer. "I would also like to keep you on staff, your salary is on the subsequent page along with my cell number. I will be in town for another day. Think it over and call me tomorrow evening. Business isn't for everyone, Ward, sometimes it's best to be an employee." Then, Goldman shook his hand and strutted back out the door.

Ward continued to stare speechlessly as he watched Goldman depart. Still processing, he looked over the numbers once again. "Half a million is more than enough to pay off the mortgage and lost interest. A salary of $50,000 is comfortable for an assistant manager too. Who would the manager be? Probably another big city shyster like him," Ward thought to himself. That sour feeling returned as he recalled the arrogance from the previous conversation. However, thinking of being debt free was like thinking of a weight being lifted off his back.

Feeling a slight sense of relief, Ward did not want to return to the daily grind and fall back into negativity. Rather, he headed to the one place where he always felt free. It was 5:30, and if his calculations were correct, he could watch the last half hour of football practice. He positioned himself on the end of the sidelines just as the daily scrimmage began.

Mixed emotions ran through Ward's veins. Paying little attention to the practice, he dazed off and contemplated the decision. "Well, if it isn't the legend himself," a familiar voice clearly directed his statement right at Ward. It was Ace. "I haven't seen you in a while. Thought you might be too busy with your new goal of dominating the restaurant business. You have it all figured out yet?"

"No, I just came to think. I was just..."

Ace interrupted, "Offered a deal on the business."

Shockingly Ward muttered, "How did you find that out? It just happened."

To which the mentor casually replied, "I talked to Walt Goldman this morning, and he said he was going to speak with you today. He sounded pretty confident, but he always likes to disguise his arrogance."

Ward was confused, "How do you know Mr. Goldman? I just met him..."

Ace cut him off again, "Walt has been 'big-timing' people for years. He is a retired NFL agent. Now, he goes around buying people out and putting his name on everything. He called me when I finished college and said that I was never going to make it in the NFL. Acting like my friend, he said he could get me a spot on the practice squad though. That one phone call made me so indignant that I was determined to prove him wrong. He felt shamefaced and now he likes to keep tabs on my whereabouts. He came to my house today just to show off his new Mercedes. A lot of good that car will do him in Montana. Oh, and I can't stand his fake radio voice."

The coincidence was setting in, and Ward was trying to figure it all out. "Anyway, I think I am going to accept the offer, but I just wanted to think about it for a second."

Then, Ace calmly asked, "Well, how would this move effect your goal?"

Ward paused for a moment, "Well, my goal for the restaurant, um, is..."

Again, Ace interrupted, "You mean to tell me that you don't have a goal? After seeing first hand the power of goals, you of all people should know that you need to have goals and principles in every facet of life." Just like old times, Ace shared his vast knowledge and philosophy.

"Ward, right now you are reacting emotionally, and for the short-term in the moment. Have you ever read *The Seven Habits of Highly Effective People* by Steven Covey? Covey explains 'principle-centered living' and how important it is to have standards and principles clearly defined so your decisions can be automatic based off of your rational thoughts instead of your emotions. Sometimes, you need to think with your head instead of your heart."

Ward had forgotten how wise Ace was and how he missed the talks they used to have. "It just seems like such a relief to have someone take care of all my debts," Ward defended.

"Let's go inside for a moment; it's getting dark," Ace said. Practice ended and Ward heard a freshmen player run past him complaining about playing in the dark, and practice running late. He laughed to himself as he recalled having that same feeling time and time again.

"Give it a little time and he will understand," Ward said to Ace. All of a sudden, Ward realized that he was doing the same thing as the young player.

"Don't forget what you are living for. There is a progression to success Ward, but certain rules apply to every issue. When you define what you are working for, live it."

Chapter 15

A RACE WITHOUT A DEFINITE GOAL IS LIKE SPRINTING IN PLACE

"Hide not your talents. They for use were made. What's a sundial in the shade?" Benjamin Franklin

Ace continued the lesson. "It is tempting to make a decision that will ease a short-term pain. On the other hand, it is much wiser to foresee the long-term benefit and fight through the pain. Seth Godin calls this getting through 'the dip.' "

Not entirely convinced, Ward stated, "I am not sure if that applies to me though. I mean my business is on its last leg."

Chuckling, Ace replied, "A one-legged business? That's a sad sight, and not a happy picture to paint for your business. Tony Robbins would simply say that you need to change the metaphor you designated. Instead of being on its last leg, think of it as just about ready to get the braces off of its legs." Ward began to understand, and Ace finished. "Our mind's dominant language is not words but images, and we use metaphors to put words into images."

Ace's reference to books made Ward realize how little reading he had been doing. "Have you read that book from Robbins, Ward?"

Sheepishly, Ward announced, "I sort have fallen off the wagon when it comes to reading."

"That happens to everyone, Ward. It is only important you jump back on the wagon. Try the metaphor Jim Rohn once said, "Some people read so little, they have rickets of the mind." That is sad but true. Now, if you are ready to put some extra horsepower in your wagon, go home and set a goal for your business, tell Goldman to take a hike and let's meet tomorrow afternoon. I have the golden ticket that will take your business to the world you envisioned."

Chapter 16

A NEW GOAL WITH AN OLD FRIEND

"Many men go fishing all of their lives without knowing it is not fish they are after." Henry David Thoreau

The telephone rang. "Walt Goldman here."

"Mr. Goldman, this is Ward Young."

A sigh came from the other end of the phone, "So, I see you have come to the realization my offer is the only solution. I knew you wouldn't wait until tomorrow. You can drop the papers off at the..."

Ward interrupted, "It's not what you think. I am calling to say thanks, but I was doing just fine by myself."

Goldman cleared his throat. "You will never make it without me."

"You said the same thing about Mason Hauser. I am sure that you mean well, but I am just not interested at this time. Thanks." In the silence, Ward hung up.

"Just like old times," Ward thought as he walked into the coach's offices. "I wonder why Ace always wants to meet here instead of his house," he said to himself. When he walked into Coach Van Nest's office, Ace wasn't there, but there was a piece of paper on the clean desk, clearly placed there by Ace.

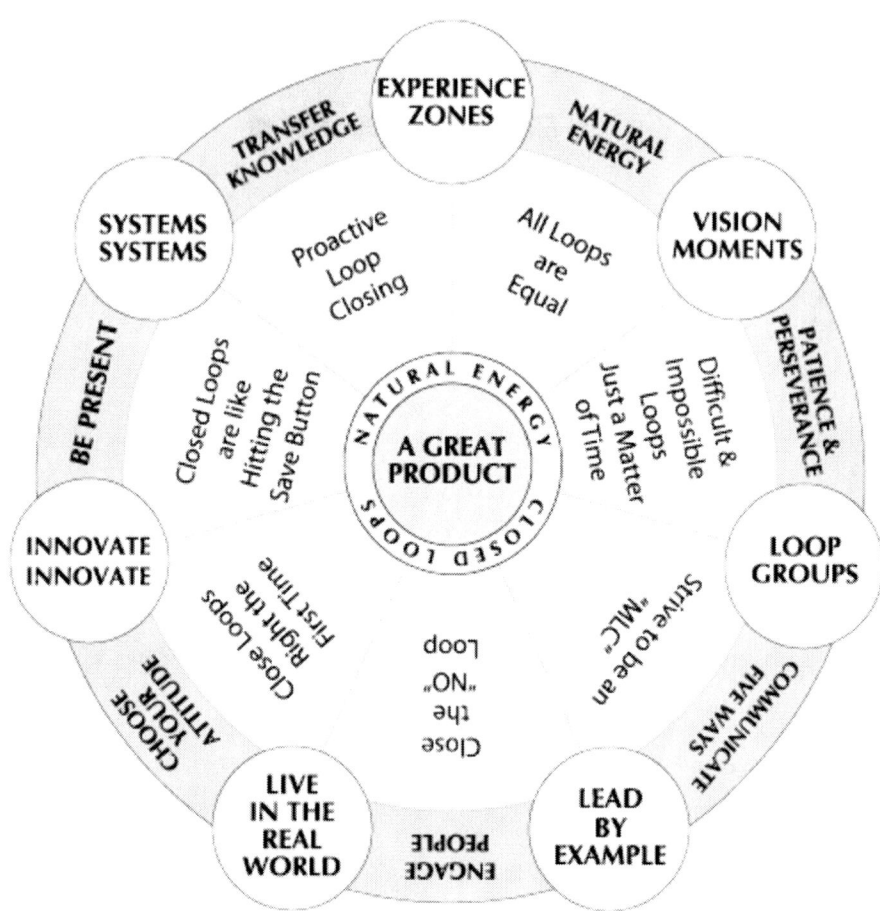

LoopOgram

"I see you've found the *loopOgram*," Ace said entering the room.

"It looks just like the *goalOgram*," Ward commented.

"Ah, yes, the basic model hasn't changed, but the content is specific to a small business. The *goalOgram* is only a small part of the bigger picture, Ward. You can use this template for anything you want to do. Just fill in the blanks, and you can solve any problem. Let's take a look at this one, I bet you can guess where we are going to start."

Ward nodded in agreement. "Experience Zones I bet. I am eager to hear this lesson."

Chapter 17

A NEW PERCEPTION OF A BUSINESS

"It's what happens to your customers as they travel through your business that, in fact, defines your business." Mike Chaet

"I haven't always been a football player, Ward. After my years in the NFL, I went on to run a couple of businesses. You ever hear of Fuego Fitness?"

Ward's eyes lit up, "You started Fuego?" Of course, he had heard. Fuego was only the largest health club chain in Montana.

"Yes, I established it and helped build it up. I have since sold the business but remain a consultant to keep my skills fresh." Ace was full of depth. Although he had known him for many years, Ward was continually impressed by his superior accomplishments.

"That's enough about me, let's talk about improving your business. Experience zones are the areas in your business under the most customer interaction. Some of them are very obvious, like the check-in area at your restaurant. Others are not so obvious, like the parking lot. Some experience zones need to be created. For example, in Fuego we created a superhero mascot, Inferno Man. He would dress with a cape and underwear on the outside of his tights. His entire job was to entertain the members of the gym, and he would go looking for gloomy people."

Eager to express his recognition of the mascot, Ward chimed in, "When I was a kid, I was at Fuego with my mom waiting in the kid's area for her to finish her workout. I had a new remote control car and was frustrated when I couldn't get it to work. 'Inferno Man' helped me fix it."

With a chuckle, Ace added, "I bet your average club wouldn't have even noticed. It's about not settling for average like a safe, boring business. If you want to be the best, you have to be profound and extraordinary. Never settle for second place in anything you do because the best businesses in the world manage their experience zones better than their competitors."

After that quick lesson, Ace's eyes glazed over in deep thought and any attentive human would be able to easily tell that an even bigger lesson was about to come. "Ward, what are you trying to accomplish with *Little Sicily*?"

"What exactly do you mean?"

"What is the difference between your restaurant and other restaurants in this town?

Ward answered without thinking, "We are the only Italian restaurant in Helena."

"I understand that, but serving different food isn't enough to be a different restaurant. If you really want to be a *Blue Ocean** in a sea of red oceans, you have to be 180 degrees different and find your niche."

* The term *Blue Ocean* was coined by W. Chan Kim and Renée Mauborgne in their international bestseller *Blue Ocean Strategy*.

Not knowing what to say, Ward asked, "What else can I do? Do you have any suggestions?"

"I do have some suggestions, and I think that you will find them to be quite obvious. However, with my suggestions there will be certain changes that you don't want to make. This is always the case with making changes. Before you reject these parts, ask yourself if your hesitation is genuine or if your mind is worried about the extra work."

That same zoned out look encompassed Ace's face for a couple of minutes before he continued. "You have a reputation in this town, Ward. Everyone knows you for being a stand up leader and a stand out player. Do you think that they are a little confused when they see you running an Italian restaurant?"

"They probably expected me to be a coach, but you are the one who told me to pursue my passion."

Nodding his head, Ace agreed, "I did tell you to pursue your passion, but I didn't tell you to forget your roots. Not so much forget your roots, but miss an opportunity."

"What opportunity did I miss?"

"The opportunity is still there. I have a question for you. Where do Carroll College fans go to eat after football games?"

"They go everywhere," Ward stated. "Some parents go to get a steak after the game, and some of the boosters go down to the Supper Club."

"What if there was one place for them to go? What if that place was your restaurant?"

Ward's face lit up with excitement as he began to ponder the innovative experiences he could create. Then, Ace handed him a piece of paper and said, "This decision is also more important than just a business decision, Ward. It is important to give back to the people and places that made you who you are. Work on this while I go grab something from my car."

Experience Zones

List your business' experience zones, and/or experiences to create.

1. The building & signs 2. Parking 3. Waiting area & method
4. Advertisements 5. Staff's attire 6. Seating 7. Waitress 8. Menu
9. Food-display 10. Food-taste 11. Price 12. Music & other sounds
13. artwork

Honestly, how is your business different from your competition, or how will you make it not only different, but better?

We will become a Carroll College Fighting Saint hotspot. We will make people's experiences the best part of their day and our name will change to - The Saint's Kitchen. We'll remain Italian specific, but our menu will expand like Italy coming to Carroll College. Each experience zone will be a unique & exciting experience never settling for average. Customers will not only see & feel Italy (statues, art, street performers, etcetera), but a Carroll College touch will be added as well.

Get in the Zone!

LOOPS 4 *YOUR* LIFE

Chapter 18

MAKE THEIR DAY*

"Never tell people how to do things. Tell them what to do and they will surprise you with their ingenuity." General George S. Patton

Returning from his car with a black book in hand, Ace said, "Looks like you are already prepared for lesson number two."

"As long as that is not the black book John Gotti had his hit list in, I'm ready."

Confused, Ace continued, "I'm not quite sure what you mean by that, but let's move on. These are my notes on Fuego; I just wanted to show you the vision statement in ink, when we first wrote it."

He opened the book to the first page reading it aloud. "It's Fuego Fitness' vision to be the best fitness community and reinvent people's perception of health clubs through creating a fun and ego-free atmosphere where people enjoy both working and exercising."

Ward eagerly added, "That is why you passed out wristbands at the football games with your vision on it."

"Exactly! We want everyone to know our vision. It is the law of attraction. Our vision becomes a self-fulfilling prophecy when it is at the forefront of everyone's behaviors. When everyone in our business is on the same page working for the

---

* First written about in the bestseller *FISH!* By Stephen C. Lundin, Ph.D., Harry Paul, and John Christensen

same ultimate endpoint, vision moments are created. Vision moments are the result of empowered employees interacting with customers, and they are the building blocks of your culture."

Ward chimed in, "Not sure if this is what you mean, but I saw a vision moment once. Your front desk worker overheard a member explaining why she couldn't make the exercise class that day because she had to run to feed her dog. The desk worker must have known where she lived because he told her not to skip the workout. He was going on break and would drive home and feed the dog for her."

Nodding his head, Ace finished the story, "These moments only happen because our workers know that it is our vision to reinvent people's perception of health clubs. We stressed this basic point and empowered the workers to capitalize on those moments. As a result, that lady will probably be a member for life."

Ace handed Ward another piece of paper and said, "The days of micromanagement are over. Employees want to feel important and to be recognized. Any fool can supervise a project by putting the fear of failure in employees, but only a seasoned vet knows to put ego aside and to trust employees with responsibility.

You already have some great ideas for the soon to be named *Saint's Kitchen*, and I know this will be a hit. Now, you must define your vision and express it in a concise couple of sentences. Make it specific also. It needs to be unambiguous and easy to understand. Southwest Airlines would call themselves 'the low fare airline.' With that statement at the forefront of everything they did, their employees were empowered to be themselves and they made their decisions with that vision at the core of their thought process."

After the long lesson, cottonmouth set in Ace's word processor. "Take your time filling this in Ward. I am going to grab glass of lemon water. I expect that you will need a glass after closing this loop also."

Vision Moments

What is the vision of your company? (if you are an existing company, allow all of your employee's input in the vision)

The Saint's Kitchen is the restaurant to eat before and after Carroll College events.

The Saint's Kitchen vision elaborated - To create an enjoyable, educational, energizing, and 'filling' experience about more than just food. We are a place where our customers & employees will be excited to show up & be glad to refer others.

"I can see clearly now the rain is gone."

LOOPS 4 *YOUR* LIFE

Vision
Moments

Describe the culture of your business. How you will get everyone to not only buy into the vision but also to live it and to expand it?

Everyone will know our vision. Awards will be given to employees & customers who can recite the 'vision' on the spot. Vision moments will be headlined in the waiting area as well as the menus. We will send coupons in the mail to locals in the community who have done a good deed or who gave someone a 'vision moment' in their own way. We will empower our employees to act on the vision and to create vision moments. Everyone's voice will be heard & considered. I will establish the Saint's Kitchen scholarship and a portion of every meal will go towards a student's education opportunity.

Persuade by the depth of your conviction rather than by the height of your logic.

LOOPS 4 *YOUR* LIFE

Chapter 19

MULTIPLY YOUR BRAINPOWER

"No two minds ever come together without creating a third, invisible, intangible force, which may be likened to a third mind."
Napoleon Hill

As Ward finished *vision moments* and devoured the lemon water, he was anxious to move on to the next loop. "Alright, Ace, tell me what *loop groups* are."

Ace looked at his watch, smiled, and said, "Grab your notes and come with me." Minutes later Ward was a passenger in Ace's green Ford Explorer. As they hurried across town, the state's Capitol building came into sight. Parking his car rather quickly, Ace jumped out and swiftly walked to the building's entrance. Ward quickened his pace to catch up. The building was vast and held some ornate pieces of art that slowed down the younger man's pursuit. Ward was surrounded by marble pillars and gold embossed tiles that would have surely made any first-timer stop and stare.

Turning a corner around which his mentor had vanished, Ward almost ran into Ace as he explained, "We are about to enter what is called an *external loop group*. It's a group of small business owners from around town who meet to share goals, visions, values, action plans, and explain how they evaluate their progress. We meet regularly to talk about the challenges we face and how these challenges can be overcome.

I love this place. The only thing better than one person's idea is two minds on the same idea." Ace added, "Follow me."

They entered one of the Capitol building's rooms to find a group of seven people circled around a table. There were two open seats. After Ace introduced his friends and all of the greetings were out of the way, Ward was able to see this Loop Group in action. A coffee shop owner spoke passionately about his new coffee bean from a tiny island off Indonesia, and how he planned to market the product. The others offered suggestions and promised they would have to try this new product and invite their friends to do the same. As everyone went around the table, the level of ideas and enthusiasm being generated astounded Ward. As the ideas were discussed, he saw average ideas morph into remarkable ideas.

All too soon, the meeting ended. The members exchanged business cards with Ward and genuinely seemed to desire his presence at the next meeting. As Ace walked Ward back to the lobby, he explained, "There is another kind of *loop group* called an Internal *loop group*, where your employees form specific groups to improve a part of the business and to better live out the business' Vision." After a quick pause, he asked, "Can you think of any *internal loop groups* for *The Saint's Kitchen*?"

Ward responded, "I'm sure I can! I have all these ideas at the front of my mind..." Looking back to the older man, he asked excitedly, "Where's the next loop?"

"Ha! That's great, Ward! Here you go." He handed the young man the next sheet. Ward grabbed one of the lobby chairs, pulled out his pen, and went to work.

Loop Groups

Why would you want to join a group of diverse, non-competing business owners, and what would you hope to gain from it?

Joining an external Loop Group is really common sense once you think about it! It's the perfect place to share resources, experiences, and information among people of a common purpose to learn and help each other succeed. I now have a vision to have a study group for the younger students in the community.

Knowing your business' Vision Statement, what is one issue or problem where an Internal Loop Group may be necessary? What will make it successful?

For The Saint's Kitchen, an ILG is necessary to create natural energy among our customers and our employees. The only way an ILG can be truly successful is if the employees feel they have a hand in creating the solution. That way, they will take ownership of the idea and it will have a better chance at succeeding.

"With our powers combined..."

LOOPS 4 *YOUR* LIFE

Chapter 20

LEARNING TO LEAD

"What you do speaks so loudly that I cannot hear what you say."
Ralph Waldo Emerson

"The only way you can tell what a person really believes is by his ACTIONS, not his words." Brian Tracy

Smiling as he put his pen down, Ward looked up to talk with Ace, but all he saw was a small piece of paper sitting on the seat opposite the lobby where the older man had been sitting. Ward walked over to it and read the scribbling, "Sorry bud, had to run. Give me a call tonight at 9:00 PM." Ward continued reading, "P.S. – Think about how you can *lead by example.*"

"Another one of his cryptic sayings," Ward mused. Waiting until the time he was to call Ace, he had plenty of time to reflect on his new situation. "How funny." He thought. "Only a day ago I was thinking I had failed, and that alligator-shoed Goldman was going to buy me out! It's amazing what a new perspective will do." Ward added to himself, "And a new education. Maybe that's why Ace seems to have all the answers. He has definitely continued seeking wisdom after he earned his college degree."

At 8:55 PM, Ward called Ace. In a light tone, the older man exclaimed, "Five minutes early!"

To which Ward quickly retorted, "Five minutes early is right on time in my book!"

Ace replied, "Ha! You're a good man, Mr. Young." Ward smiled as Ace continued. "Meet me at the Carroll College P.E. Center parking lot at 10:00 PM – or 9:55 for you! And bring your coat."

It was an all-too-common cold Montana night as Mr. Young parked next to the Ford Explorer. Mr. Hauser signaled Ward to jump into the passenger seat. "Good to see you again, Ward. Did you think about *leading by example?*"

"I did." Ward responded. "To me *leading by example* means to be out in front where my employees can see me living the vision."

"Very good. You are on the right track. There are some extra thoughts that go along with this loop, however."

Just then, Ace's gaze drifted past his passenger and Ward followed it to the entrance of the P.E. Center. He could see all the assistant coaches leaving. "What are they all doing here at this hour?" Ward asked with surprise.

"Believe it or not, Ward, it's more uncommon for those coaches to leave before 10:00 PM than it is for them to leave after. To be a college coach in any sport, a person must be truly passionate about it." Just then, the women's volleyball coach left the building. Ace opened his car door and asked for Ward to follow him. They went to the entrance of the P.E. Center, where Ace opened the door.

The lobby was dark, and the gym as well. As they made their way through the lobby, Ward noticed the unmistakable greenish hue that could only be the reflection of football film being projected in the next room. Turning the corner, the two saw Coach Van Nest watching film by himself. The brightness of the projector's image must have made Ace and Ward impossible to see in the darkened lobby since Coach simply kept on watching film. They stood there silently for several moments before Ace whispered, "Let's walk."

When they were out of earshot, Ward was speechless as he shook his head. Ace broke the silence, "You see, Ward, Coach Leads by Example. Not only does he live out the Vision of the team, but he also does so when no one is there to see him. He does it that way, every day. That is integrity: What you do when no one is looking."

Ward let those words sink in. Everyday. Even if no one saw him. That approach was much different than his image of leading his employees into battle, charging on horseback with his sword raised.

Seeming to read the young man's mind, Ace continued, "There's more to being a leader than one moment of glory. When you speak to your employees about your new ideas, many of them will have reservations whether these ideas are just the flavors of the month. People need to see that you are truly committed to something before they will be willing to commit to it." Ward was floored by these insights into leadership that he had never heard before as Ace turned on a set of lobby lights and handed him the next sheet.

Lead By Example

How will you Lead by Example and why is it important?

I will Lead by Example by living out our Vision Statement in everything that I do, and focus on creating natural energy. I will be the number one fan at every Carroll event that I can make. The Saint's Kitchen will be a part of every function as well. Leading by Example inspires others to follow a course of action and our Vision.

How can you develop your leadership and the leadership of others?

I will reward my employees for following the Vision, and give responsibility through empowering them to find their own solutions. Their Italian uniforms will also have Carroll College embroidered on the chest, and the gondoliers will wear purple and gold stripes.

Walk your Talk.

LOOPS 4 *YOUR* LIFE

Chapter 21

COMING TO TERMS WITH REALITY

"He who marches with his feet on the ground, but head in the clouds
may be surprised when the ground falls from underneath him."
Thomas Bryan Hill

Ward made certain to keep an eye on Ace this time. Mason 'Ace' Hauser silently stared outside as his student approached him. Ace turned and said, "Let's take a walk."

Moments later they were back on the football field which was slightly lit up by the stadium scoreboard. The atmosphere reminded Ward of the last time the two of them were on the field – when Ward learned about the self-triad. The scene also reminded him of his last game on the field, the heartbreaker when the Saints lost the National Championship. He felt a chill run up his spine and the cold wind accentuated the feeling.

Ace went straight to business. "The next loop is to *live in the real world*. What this loop means is successful businesses accept the world for what it is, not for what they think it should be. Too many times, owners plan and act in an imaginary world. It's great to dream big, but as Jim Collins says in his book, *Good To Great*, we must also confront the 'brutal facts' of reality."

"Okay. That idea makes sense, but what exactly does it mean?" Ward asked.

"It means when you start implementing these new ideas, you will have your doubters."

Ward interrupted, "And I understand I'll have to convince them over time through *leading by example*."

Ace countered, "That's not the whole picture unfortunately. No matter how great you lead, there will still be some employees who don't follow the vision. Even worse, they act as a cancer, negatively influencing all the other employees and customers around them. It's as Jim Collins also said, "Get the right people on the bus, in the right spots, before you start driving.""

Ward waited for Ace to elaborate and he watched him point to the field they stood on, "Think of your offensive football huddle. There's a certain order to it. The linemen are always in front with the running back in the middle of the second row and the wide receivers on each side of him. When Coach knows the right players are in the right spots, he then sends in the play call and the offense breaks to the line of scrimmage. If just one wide receiver chooses to walk casually to his spot, the offense will receive a 'delay of game' penalty. What would Coach do if someone did that?"

Ward laughed as he said, "Well, for starters, he'd kick him off the field and get someone else in there he could count on." Something clicked in Ward's mind, "Just as an owner would fire the negative employee and get the right person for the job in the right spot!"

"Very good, Ward! Now, what happens if a wide receiver gets injured?"

"Another one is always ready to go." Ward answered and then continued. "For *The Saint's Kitchen*, that would mean creating a schedule where an employee was sort of 'on call' in case something happened."

"That's called having a Plan B." Ace stated. "And what happens if Coach gets the play call to the offense late?"

Ward responded, "They might get a 'delay of game' penalty."

Ace continued, "And what happens if an employee doesn't show up for work on time?"

To which Ward concluded, "The reputation of *The Saint's Kitchen* would get a penalty, and word could spread. For us, that situation would mean creating a 15 minute overlap during times when employees switch rotations."

"That's called 'leaving margins.' " As Ace gave out the next sheet he proudly stated, "Ward, you truly understand *living in the real world.*"

The lights from the scoreboard provided enough luminance for Ward to fill out the next essential Loop.

Live in the Real World

How can you expect the unexpected and institute a Plan B?

Along with having an employee' on call', we will make sure that the waiter can fill in for the host, the busboy, and the bartender if necessary. And we will have an internal Loop Group meeting that empowers our employees to help develop a back-up plan.

How can you accept reality and leave Margins in both time and money?

Along with having a Plan B, we will have a fifteen minute overlap during employee rotations. I will also make more realistic budgets as opposed to the idealistic ones from the past. A specific' Margin Budget' will also be established.

Life isn't a scripted play. Be ready for the unsteady.

LOOPS 4 *YOUR* LIFE

Chapter 22

PUT ON YOUR RALLY CAPS

"There is no natural phenomenon more powerful than a society of people on a common journey of righteousness to help others."
Dan Jacobs-Karl

It was now past midnight and the two friends still stood on the field. Ward's hands were losing their dexterity in the cold, but he was hungry for more. "Only two more Loops to go! What's next?"

Ace slowly stated, "Actually, Ward, this is a good place to stop." The young man gave Ace a challenging look that forced him to explain, "I know you're thinking I'm testing your resolve by giving you the run-around, but I really believe this is a good place to stop for now. You have much to implement. Let's set up a meeting two months from now. Then we can finish the last two Loops." Reluctantly, Ward agreed, and they left the football field walking back to their cars, calling it a night.

Over the next few weeks Ward began to truly understand how challenging this new process was. He was lucky his assiduous manager, Mary, believed in the changes. The name was officially changed to *The Saint's Kitchen*, and the entire restaurant transformed into a hall of fame for Carroll College athletics.

A student-tutoring program was established and dozens of parents dropped their grade-schoolers off for free tutoring with

Carroll College students after school. Many parents would often grab a bite to eat at the same time.

Just like Ace said, some employees weren't quite as excited as Mary. In one meeting, a waitress asked, "What do we *have* to do now?"

Ward was taken aback, but before he could respond, Mary chimed in: "You don't have to do anything extra. All that this means is *we get* to have more fun and more of a say on what goes on around here. What isn't there to like about that?"

The waitress said, "Actually... that sounds pretty good."

Mary also took it upon herself to head up the *energy loop group*, an Internal Loop Group designed to create a fun, educational, and energizing experience for both employees and customers. Ward thought to himself, "She's definitely the right person in the right spot!" Also, a group of servers chose to form the *experience zones loop group*.

After a few weeks, both groups gave reports to the entire staff on ideas for improving *The Saint's Kitchen*. Mary started, "Our team has come up with some really exciting ideas for living out *The Saint's Kitchen* vision." Mary went on to discuss the role of eye contact in making a connection with someone. She recommended capturing each customer's full name, phone number, and mailing address when they wanted to make a reservation. This way, when they came into the restaurant, the greeter could boom enthusiastically, "Hello, John Bartholomew

Smith! Please follow me." Afterwards, *The Saint's Kitchen*
would mail a 'Free Saint's Gift with Meal' certificate to their
homes. Lastly, the *energy loop group* recommended asking
customers the specific phrase, "How may I serve you?"

A younger waiter who was currently going to college stood
up to speak on *experience zones*. "Our *loop group* realized
experience zones are everywhere. So, for the time being, we
decided to focus on attire, artwork, and lighting." The waiter
illuminated how dressing like Italian waiters, hanging artwork
on the walls, and dimming the lights would all help to heighten
the experience.

Ward smiled as he sat among the enthusiastic employees
of *The Saint's Kitchen*. Over the next several weeks, everything
seemed to be getting better and better. Business was at an all-
time high, employees were happy, and so were the customers.
Reservations now had to be made hours in advance to ensure a
spot. Ward was busier than ever, but he was enjoying the extra
hours he spent maintaining all the new ideas and programs his
employees presented. Caught up in the various tasks, Ward
almost forgot to call Ace at the end of two months. Calling his
mentor, Ward filled Ace in on all the restaurant's
developments. Ace sounded happy as he said, "Well, I think
now is a good time to show you the final two loops."

Chapter 23

FINDING NEW WAYS TO INNOVATE

"We must understand the tight protective grip of the norm in order to appreciate the methods of escape."
Stephen C. Lundin

"No one goes there anymore. It's too crowded."
Yogi Berra

After parking his car downtown and paying the meter next to it, Ward walked over to the familiar Ford Explorer on the side of the street. Moments later Ward and Ace were catching up as they passed through the downtown walking mall. "So, what's the next loop, Ace?" the student asked.

Continuing to walk, Ace explained. "The next loop is to innovate. Innovation is the lifeblood of any business."

"But how does that thought apply to *The Saint's Kitchen*? We are doing really well right now. Why should I change a good thing?" Ward asked.

"There is no such thing as staying the same, Ward. Either you are innovating your business or you are losing momentum to your competition. I don't mean to change all your recipes and become an Irish Pub, but I do mean customers are dynamic and they have ever-changing needs." Ace allowed Ward to think on his words as he said, "Come over here."

The two walked into a local tea store. Immediately the lady working the front desk exclaimed with a smile, "You two look like the type who enjoy a good cup of tea!"

"We do!" Ace replied. Almost immediately Ward was being handed a delicious cup of tea as the lady showed Ace and Ward around the shop, putting teas and lotions in Ward's free hand and saying, "Your Mom'll love this one!"

Leaving the store, Ward had a smile on his face and $25 of teas and lotions already gift-wrapped. He said, "Hey, what a great place! They had quality *experience zones.*"

Ace commented, "You know, it wasn't always like that. I remember when the store first opened. It was struggling to survive until the owner had a wonderful idea. She decided to always have a hot pot of tea ready to serve for each customer who walked through the door. She wanted them to *experience* what her product was, not just hear about it. Her innovation saved the business, and now it's thriving." Ace turned the subject back to Ward's business. "Though *The Saint's Kitchen* is prospering, you must always be thinking of ways to innovate or else you will end up where you were just two months ago."

Ward thought back to two months ago. It seemed like a distant memory. He understood Ace and realized that even though he felt safe with his business, he must always plan for his own obsolescence.

Innovate

Why is it vital to always Innovate? List areas in your business that need Innovation.

If I stop trying to get better, I'll actually be getting worse while my competition gets better. While we have pictures on the wall, the whole Italian experience can definitely improve.

List ways you can Innovate those areas in the near future?

To improve the Italian experience we will get a big statue of the David at the entrance, and David will be wearing a Carroll College football helmet. Also, the greeters could be different Italian characters (like a chef, a fancy waiter, or gondolier with Carroll College colors. These innovations will immediately get customers' In the Zone!'

Think outside the box... What box?

LOOPS 4 *YOUR* LIFE

Chapter 24

SYSTEMS BUILD CONSISTENCY

"Management works in the system;
Leadership works on the system." Steven R. Covey

Just as soon as Ward finished writing, the final loop was forced fed from the 'wise one.' "This final lesson is the icing to the cake," Ace explained. "All you have done will vanish in time if your work cannot be replicated. Systemization is the catapult that launches a great business past the average ones. If you want to evolve and to expand as a person and as a business, you must adopt the philosophy you will 'do it right the first time' and then standardize what you have just done. People waste a ton of time doing the same project over and building similar campaigns from scratch."

Ward interjected, "But I don't feel as confident in some people's work."

Ace replied with a nod, "Ah, yes, that is the number one form of resistance and justification holding these average businesses back. Some people might not be as good at certain things as you are, but I guarantee you will work yourself into the ground if you don't invent a system easy enough to follow so your staff will rank close to your efforts." Understanding of Ace's last advice entered Ward's mind.

"Also, you may do great work, but if you don't have a system, I bet you work varies from time to time. Have you ever

97

ordered your favorite dish at another restaurant, and it wasn't quite the same, or it wasn't as good as the last time?"

The student agreed, "Yes."

Then the teacher continued, "Such inconsistency kills the very culture you are trying to create. 'Sometimes excellent' is worse than 'consistently good'." Ace politely nabbed a teabag from Ward's recent purchase and elaborated on the subject.

"In strictly business terms, regardless of nutrition or other controversies, McDonalds has built their empire on this philosophy. No matter what McDonalds in the world you go to, a burger tastes the same. They built a system so easy and perfect that nearly anyone can cook a burger which always tastes the same."

The young entrepreneur added, "That's so true, and we need to do the same. We just need to be careful not to decrease the value or to make it 'generic.' But to standardize our processes. I bet my employees will have more time to focus on the other loops as well."

There is no satisfaction greater to a teacher than when the student teaches him the lesson. Ace finished, "Absolutely, with less tedious tasks, your staff will have more time and energy to focus on *vision moments* and *experience zones*." With a beckoning motion to Ward, signaling him to start writing, he said, "Let's close this final loop."

Systems

Discuss why standardization is important in your business and what tasks of higher value it will allow you to work on.

Standardization will allow myself and my staff to spend more time with our customers. We can start working on the business rather than in the business. We will all be happier when we can do what we love rather than redundant and tedious tasks.

Free up the Creative Spirit.

LOOPS 4 *YOUR* LIFE

Systems

List everywhere you have seen and can add standardization to your business.

I will systematize everything. From the way our staff answers phones to how our bussers clean up. I will even standardize the path and reaction our customers take to our scenery and artwork. I will also systematize the approach we used to create a sport-specific restaurant. If need be, this system can be followed in other areas with communities that revolve around colleges and sports teams. We already do a good job with our back office systems (books, agreements, etc.). We will offer a system of how our waitresses recite the menu. The system will be in place, but also allow leniency for our staff to act as themselves and carryout our vision.

Hey partner, if you ain't on systems, the systems will be on you.

LOOPS 4 *YOUR* LIFE

Chapter 25

ALWAYS MOVE FORWARD

"I love running cross country... On a track, I feel like a hamster." Robin Williams

Only three months passed by since Ward put the finishing touches on the last loop, and he was a whole new person. *The Saint's Kitchen* was functioning amazingly on the new systems, and the restaurant seemed to get better everyday. The newly anointed businessman was even negotiating a few contracts in the surrounding cities to open branch restaurants.

Holding true to a promise he made, Ward pulled his car up to Ace's small bachelor house. Before he could even apply the parking break on, the passenger door opened. "Someone's in a hurry," Ward said to his spiffed up mentor. He proceeded, "Is that cologne I smell."

Coming from the maxed out smile of Ace was an eager sincerity, "I've been waiting for this moment since you promised me three months ago. I don't get out much."

A moment of silence filled the car. Then Ward broke the quiet, "Yeah, we have just been insanely busy at the restaurant. You know what I mean. I am up to my ears with all of the expanding we have been doing. It's good though. It sure beats the alternative. Right?"

The corners of Ace's lips lowered a bit, "You bet. It's good to be making money. In the process of it all, just make sure to make time for what matters to you. And don't miss the point."

With quick nods of his head, Ward gave the impression he understood, "Oh, yeah, I love it. I love what I do, and I don't mind working extra hours."

Ace changed the subject, "I saw you with a girl the other day. How is that relationship going?"

To which the young man replied, "Oh, you mean Sophia? Yeah, she's great; we've been dating for a couple of months now."

The elder bachelor cracked, "Sounds like you won't be needing any of this cologne if you've already got the wife picked out."

Ward immediately defended himself, "Don't go jumping to any conclusions. I am way too busy to be starting any families at this point. I really like her but I'm just so focused on success right now." Ace tried to respond, but the driver was too busy parallel parking to listen.

The restaurant was so packed they were forced to park five blocks away. Despite the other eateries, the streets were quiet as they walked past empty offices retired for the day. The moon was dark, but the lights of *The Saint's Kitchen* over-illuminated everything else.

They walked into the newly remodeled atrium where a replica of Michelangelo's Florentine sculpture the 'David' was the center of attention, gold football helmet and all. Before they even reached the hostess stand, a purple and gold striped shirted man who looked like a gondolier greeted them both. "You must be Ace," said the handsome man.

Ward introduced them. "Ace, this is one of our best hands, Zack Bartlett. Zack, this is the man, the myth, the legend, Mason Hauser."

They shook hands, "Ah, don't believe any stories this guy tells you, and please call me Ace."

With a booth already waiting in the back, Zack led the two comrades to their seats where a bottle of champagne was waiting. As soon as the fizz evaporated, Ace proposed a toast. "I must say I am very proud of you and your consistency to yet another transition." With a clink and a drink, Ace continued to a different conversation. "Now, I am looking forward to getting paid for my consultations with some gnocchi and tortellini. I bet that you're glad you didn't let Walt Goldman take all this away."

Ward held his glass up, "I'll drink to that."

Then Ace changed his tone again, "I want you to think about something, Ward. Think about how you have matured since starting up the business, and then think about the maturation process of your football career."

The pupil added, "Yeah, I finally discovered how to accomplish something meaningful in life and not just conference championships."

Putting his hand out as if to cut him off, Ace redirected his point. "A successful business is of no more value than a championship. Each has its time and place. I want you to understand there is a *progression to success* and that progression is the secret to maturing. True success gets its value from within you and only you. A person needs to plan for the future, but that person must also strive for the moment. At that moment, football was most important to you. And, at this moment, your business is most important. I know that it's hard to perceive, but you will have different priorities in the future. Try to open your mind, to prepare and to realize a transition or shift will come again. You don't want to get to be my age and try to change something when it's too late.

Remember these three things: one: always work towards something. Two: don't focus so much on the finish line that you miss the scenery of the race. And three: progress your life and goals. A senior citizen has no right at a high school dance."

Ace's hand went down, and he took a sip of champagne. Ward followed, "Wow, I have never had a motivational speech for an upcoming meal before, but I liked it." Though he had been listening, it was apparent Ward didn't understand the plot of Ace's teaching.

Chapter 26

FAMILY MATTERS

"The happiest moments of my life have been the few which I have passed at home in the bosom of my family." Thomas Jefferson

The three-hour meal hit an abrupt halt when Ward looked at his watch. "Whoa, look at that. I had better get you home. It is getting late."

Finishing his last bite of gnocchi, Ace replied, "Relax I don't have anywhere to be. It's not like I have a wife to answer to. I come and go as I please."

Slowing his mind down for a second, Ward added, "I just realized I have never asked if you were ever married."

With a solemn look, the forty-five year old declared, "That is not something I am proud of Ward. The older I get, the more I regret not settling down earlier. I had a serious girlfriend once. We had a kid together."

Ward looked surprised. "You never said you had a kid."

Picking up where he left off, Ace continued, "We were together all the way through college and three years following. After my run in the league, she got pregnant and I got scared. Looking back, running away was a huge mistake in my life. I was too selfish to marry her. Heck, I never even got a chance to meet my own son."

Ward attempted to pick him up, "I'm sorry, but maybe she wasn't your soul mate."

Ace shook his head. "Love isn't some emotion like Hollywood makes it to be Ward. Love is an act that you do, and you have to give love in order to receive it. I had a great thing, but I stopped giving to it. When you stop feeding the fire, it burns out."

Struggling to think of something to say, Ward responded, "Nonetheless, think of all the good times you had and all the accomplishments you made. You are only forty-five, and you have accomplished more than most people in their late sixties."

That same solemn look drooped lower each second. "Accomplishments are great, but they are short-lived unless you have a partner to share them."

That same misunderstood reply came from the youngster as he put on his jacket, signaling that the meal had ended, "You have shared you accomplishments with me though, and you have also shared your knowledge with me. I mean, I wouldn't have made it here without your guidance."

Following the cue, Ace grabbed his coat and slipped a hefty tip in Zack Bartlett's apron. "I have taught you much, and you have always listened very well. You must understand this is another lesson. I am very proud of you, and I want you to achieve all of your desires in the business world. It is hard to foresee yourself having solemn feelings now, but I just want you to use your peripherals occasionally and don't miss the point."

Ward was clearly listening, but he was walking briskly as they made their way out the front door. "Sorry, I just had to make the exit quick so I didn't force myself into working overtime. Sofia tells me that I need to learn to unwind sometimes. I know I'm young and I have much to learn, but I understand what you are saying. I am just so focused on being successful now. I want to get there first and then start a family."

Ace grabbed Ward by the shoulder, "Humans are goal driven beings, Ward, and it is an absolute necessity that we have something to strive for. However, your life will be brutally empty if all you have are your accomplishments. Remember this, and always try to enjoy the moment called 'now.' " Pulling a *Saint's Kitchen* matchbook from his pocket he wrote on the back and handed it to Ward.

"If you are always trying to be somewhere you are not, you will never be where you are."

Chapter 27

DON'T MISS THE POINT

"Life is like dancing. If we have a big floor, many people will dance. Some will get angry when the rhythm changes. But life is changing all the time." Don Miguel Ruiz

Papers flew through the air and drawers were slammed as Ward fumbled through his home office desk in a mad rush. "Where the hell did I put that certificate?" He said to himself. "Ah, last place I thought to look." An old matchbook caught his eye when he finally found the certificate, the same matchbook that Ace had given him nearly nine years ago.

It had been a while since he last opened it up. Despite already running ten minutes behind schedule, he paused for a brief moment to read Ace's words of wisdom.

"If you are always trying to be somewhere you are not, you will never be where you are."

Throwing the matchbook into his pocket, he ran out to his minivan where his wife, Sophia, and two children, Megan and Steve, were patiently waiting. "Come on, babe, we don't ever get to go out as a family, and when we do, you are always late." Sophia stated. "Did you, at least, find the certificate with the directions on it?" He chose not to respond, but instead waved the certificate in the air. The tardy van then departed to an alumni reunion at a new eatery on the outskirts of town.

"Is Uncle Ace going to be there, Dad?" his eight-year-old daughter asked. "I have a book report to trade him." Ace didn't give typical gifts to Ward's children. Instead, he would give them a book and later trade them money for a brief report describing what they had learned.

"I'm sure he will be waiting for you, Sweetie." Megan's mother replied since Ward was apparently typing an email on his cell phone. "What about you Steve? Did you write a report for Uncle Ace?"

Though he was a year younger than Megan, Steve was much too competitive to be out done by his older sister. He would always strive to meet her every step. "Right here." Steve said as he pulled a folded piece of paper from his pocket.

"You know, we should invite him over for dinner soon. We haven't done that in a long time. I can't even remember the last time the two of you spent more than ten minutes together. When would be a good time?" Sophia asked the distracted passenger as she tried to read the directions on the certificate and drive at the same time. "Ward? Are you listening?"

He stopped typing for a second, "Oh, yeah, of course. One second, just let me finish this email."

After a final turn, she threw the directions on the floor in relief as the minivan rolled into a free parking space at the end of the lot. Ward's email conveniently finished simultaneously.

He returned his phone to the holster. "We could have just walked from the house if we are going to park this far away."

An annoyed stare shot back his way as Sophia answered, "Next time, when you drive, you can park wherever you want."

Ward grabbed her and gave her a hug. "Babe, I am sorry, I was just trying to joke with you." They gave each other a brief kiss on the lips in forgiveness and hurried inside to the banquet.

That rushed car ride, borderline argument, and Band-Aid makeup was a pinpoint summary of Ward's family life. For the most part, they spent time together and acted like a quintessential couple. Although they were together physically, there was still a sort of disconnect. One could even say they were together mentally since they did have the normal family conversations. However, just like typical families in this day and age, they weren't really living in the moment.

Chapter 28

AN UNWELCOME SURPRISE

"Too busy thinking about tomorrow's sunrise, today's light falls to shadow, leaving us in continual darkness." D.P. Jones

The reunion dinner was not what Ward expected. Although the food was fine and the conversation pleasant, he could tell Ace had something on his mind. The older man insisted on paying for the meal, and before he said goodbye to Megan and Steve, he gave both of them their own big twirl in the air. As they stood in the lobby, Ward told Sophia he'd meet them at the car in a moment. He turned to Ace to begin speaking, but before he could say anything, Ace grabbed his shoulder and spoke. "I'm not well, Ward. I'm dying." Ward looked for something in Ace's expression to indicate that he wasn't serious. He found nothing. The older man held his gaze and continued, "Bladder cancer. It's one of those things. Doctor says we didn't catch it in time. He says I have two weeks."

Ward felt something well up from deep within, as he struggled to contain it. Here he was, face to face with his mentor, his second father, his friend. The well reached his eyes, but both men maintained their stare. There was so much that Ward wanted to say, but he couldn't find the willpower to speak without crying. From outside, the horn from the minivan snapped Ward from his thoughts. Ace came in softly, "Go to your family. You don't need to say anything. I know how you feel. If you get a chance in the next couple of days, I would like for you to come over to my house. I have been working on something. Something that has been missing in my life, and I don't want you to have the same regrets." Wiping his eyes, Ward nodded in assurance and headed to the car.

The car ride back home was quite different than the first. Silent and lost in his own thoughts, Ward tried to hide the tears welling in his eyes as he thought about all the times with his mentor and best friend. Although his family sensed something was wrong, Ward's actions made it apparent that he needed some time alone.

Chapter 29

DON'T LEAVE LIFE WITH THE SONG STILL IN YOU

"Every man's life ends the same way. It is only the details of how he lived and how he died that distinguish one man from another." Ernest Hemingway

Ward spent the next two days of the weekend prepping *The Saint's Kitchen* to run smoothly without him. He scheduled himself off for the next two weeks so he could be with Ace. He was thankful to have Zack Bartlett be so willing to step into the duties as Regional Manager for that time. Ward was also glad Sophia understood she wouldn't be seeing much of him the next two weeks.

With his affairs finally in order, Ward called Ace to announce he would be on his way. It wasn't Ace who answered. "Hello. This is Mr. Hauser's estate planner, Ellen Roberts. I am sorry to tell you Mr. Hauser died in his sleep last night."

Suddenly, that same welling feeling hit Ward tenfold like an unsuspecting blow to the stomach. He never even got a chance to say goodbye. The conversation continued with Ms. Roberts explaining that Ace had left some of his possessions for Ward, and he would need to pick them up some time this week. It all seemed so formal, so unemotional. Ward felt like he was above his own body, watching himself say, "Okay" over and over to the estate planner. He finished the call by saying, "I'll come straight over."

Ward hadn't seen the interior of Ace's house in all the years he'd known him. It was simple and clean. The walls were mostly bare except for a few abstract pictures of art, a younger Ace in a Denver Broncos' jersey, and a picture of himself and Ace smiling at each other after Ward won his final home game at Carroll College. Ms. Roberts led Ward to a closed room at the end of a short hallway. "Upon his passing, Mr. Hauser has stated everything in this room belongs to Ward Young." Ward creaked open the door slowly. The room was small and not as clean as the rest of the house. Papers and books were overflowing on the shelves that lined the sides of the room. At the end of the room was a desk with a single, hard, wooden chair. "Mr. Hauser has instructed you are to have this key to the house. For the next month, you can come and go as you please. At the end of the month, we ask that you have transported the contents of this room to your own property." With that, Ms. Roberts left Ward to the library and study area of his deceased mentor.

Ward scanned the room, impressed by Ace's large book collection. On the right shelf near the bottom were several binders titled, "Business loopOgrams". Above those were even more binders titled, "goalOgrams." "So, this is where it all happened." Ward thought to himself with a slight smile forming on his face. He went over and tried out the chair. "Not too comfortable," he thought. From there, his eyes glanced over the paper-strewn desk and stopped on a manila folder with two words written on it, "To Ward." Feeling his heart jump, Ward slowly grabbed the folder and opened it:

Not the most comfortable chair, is it? I really should get a new one, but I guess it's too late for that. Well, Ward, since you're reading this, I have gone to that next place, whatever that may be. It all happened suddenly. I want you to know you have a most special place in my heart. And don't worry! I know you feel the same towards me.

Ward, learning that my days are numbered made me reflect on my life. I've lived a very good life by most anyone's standards. I've had a successful athletic career, several successful businesses, and many good friends. But now that my end is upon me, I feel that I missed something. There's something else out there that can lead to a better life than I've had. An even happier, more fulfilled life. I've sensed it at times. Looking back, I feel that I might have dodged my happiest moments.

I started my final loopOgram Ward, but I cannot finish it. My hours are numbered, but it puts the biggest smile on my face knowing that you have what it takes to complete it.

You've given me more than you may ever know, Ward. Thank You.

> *Ace*

This time there was no holding back. Tears streamed down Ward's face in the study room of his deceased friend. Elbows on the desk, with his head lowered between his hands, Ward sobbed.

After some time had passed, Ward raised his head back to the manila folder on the desk. Seeing the second sheet of paper patiently waiting behind Ace's message, Ward took a deep breath and revealed his friend's final project.

LIFEOGRAM

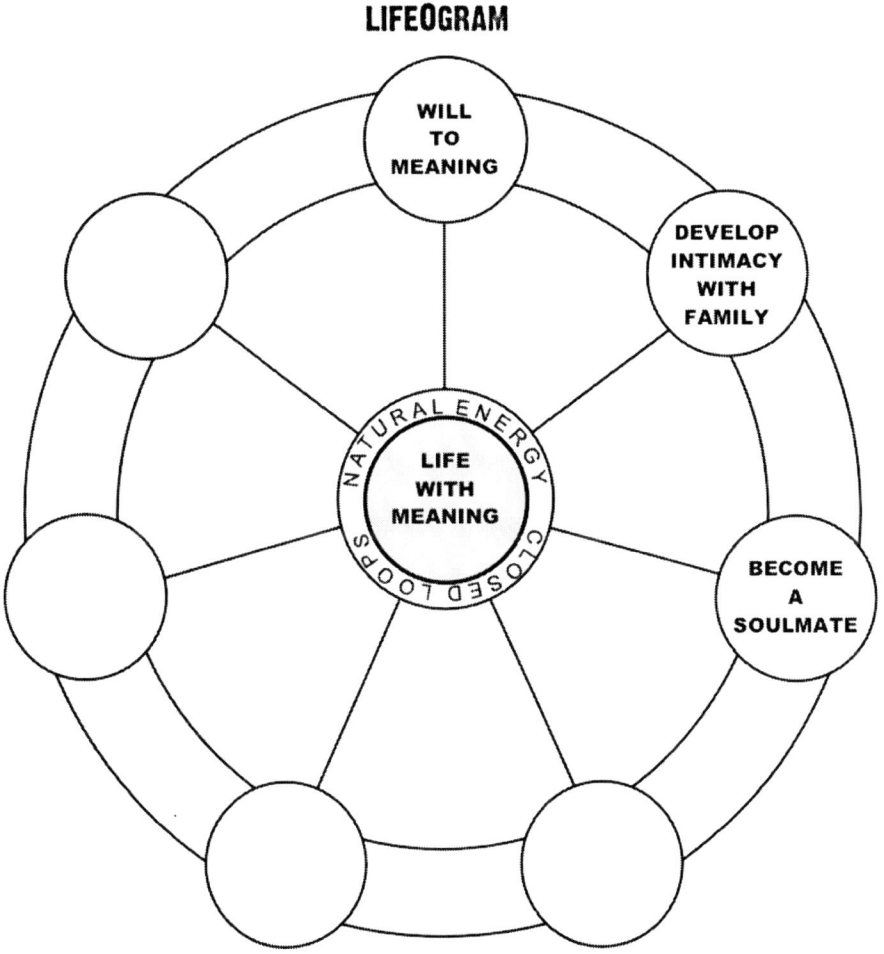

Chapter 30

MORE TO LIFE

"True religion is real living; living with all one's soul, with all one's goodness and righteousness." Albert Einstein

Though it was not even close to being finished, there was something immaculate about Ace's words. Ward thought to himself, "This is what Ace has been trying to tell me all along. Don't miss the point. I get it now." Looking down, he exposed a final note from Ace taped to the first loop.

> *This project is still incomplete Ward. Looking back on my life, it has been great. However, it is important to keep progressing and sculpting your own character. I believe this project is the missing third loopogram, and you are the only one I can think to finish it. Trust your intuition and the loops will unveil themselves. This third loopogram holds the key to life itself.*

Removing the note from the paper, Ward read the following lesson from the first loop.

Will
to
Meaning

Meaning is unique for each individual. What principles guide your life and what significance do you strive to live by and for?

Viktor Frankl has said that the primary motivation of one's life is to find meaning. In searching for meaning in my life, I have found three principles that I live my life by and for.

1) Find the good in every person and every thing. I strive to seek and understand the good and show respect to all of earth.

2) Always Have Righteous Intentions. In life, business and all interactions I will always do what is best for both parties and never intend negativity on anyone or thing.

3) Serve all that is around You. In every situation, I will always ask the golden question. How may I serve you?

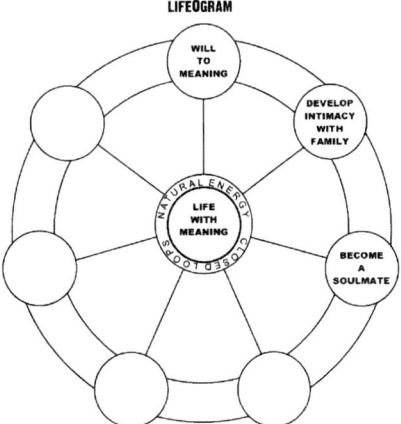

LIFEOGRAM

What does life mean to you?

LOOPS 4 *YOUR* LIFE

His tears had now dried as he eased from the chair and walked around looking at the piece of verbal art.

"Ace only finished the first loop, 'will to meaning.' There is no writing for the other two, 'family' or 'become a soul mate.' He gave the other loops a title, but never had the time to write in his definitions. Poor Ace. He had lived such a successful life in so many ways, but he was missing so much." That thought sparked a revealed sense of reality that made him rush to his car and hurry to his own house.

Chapter 31

FAMILY PRINCIPLES

"In the same way as a business, a family cannot reach its potential without everyone living the same well-defined vision."

Dan Jacobs-Karl

Nearly sprinting in the house he burst through the door calling his wife in a winded yell. "Sophy!"

Matching Ward's speed, she ran down the stairs. "What is it? What happened? Are you alright?"

Realizing he had scared her, Ward calmed his tone. "Sweetie, I have been missing the point."

Now confused, Sophia questioned, "What point?"

"The point to life, to my life. Ace left me this." He showed her the diagram and continued. "I have been distant from you and the kids, and I am so sorry. I have been so focused on my success and accomplishments I failed to appreciate the important things in life. Ace helped me progress to the level he achieved, but he is hinting that there is another lesson. A lesson that he had not learned."

Sophia sat Ward down on the couch. "You have been very good to me, and you are a great father. There is no one that I would rather be with."

"I have been a decent husband and father, but I think that I can be so much better, and a new progressive shift will create a closeness among our whole family few people reach. Some people say, 'if it's not broke, don't fix it.' I say, 'break it, and build it better.' Ace talked about living by guided principles and I think it is time we set some principles as a family. Let's get Steve and Megan to come here. I have an idea, and I want everyone to take part in it."

The children were gathered for the family meeting, the first of their young lives. A little unsure at first, the children were pleasantly surprised as they watched their dad guide the meeting and show more attentiveness than he had ever shown before.

Ward pulled out a piece of paper and made a big loop on it. "Alright, guys, we are going to line out a rough draft to our family mission statement."

"Family what?" Megan asked.

"Mission statement," her mother kindly replied. "We are going to define as a family what is most important to us and what principles we are going to live for and by."

Steve was clearly confused, "What are principles?"

Understanding the need to explain in further detail and in terms that a seven and eight year old could comprehend, Ward redefined his intentions. "Think of this as creating our own rules to a game. The game we are playing is called *Family*. We play 'family' every time we are together, every second we are together. The rules or guidelines, we're going to make up together, will be how we live our lives. We also are playing the game when we are not only with our own family, but also with other people or even by ourselves because we are always representing our family."

Megan and Steve began to see a clearer picture, and Sophia reiterated, "We are going to begin to play a game that never ends. How does that sound?" Neither child answered, but both expressed their opinions with massive smiles.

Ward then finished, "And the best part about this game is we get to make our own rules."

The meeting ended by asking each other precisely worded questions, and the entire family engaged and responded. As the night waned, they had a great time at the kitchen table. They told stories, laughed and each enjoyed a cup of Sophia's famous, sugar-free, homemade hot cocoa.

When they laid in bed that evening, Ward looked at the draft of the family loop they all worked meticulously to create. "You know, Sophy, I haven't had this much fun in a long time. I am glad we did this, and I am glad the kids helped. They are more likely to practice and to live by principles they helped make."

He gave her a kiss on the cheek, and she said, "I feel like we have really taken a big progression forward as a family tonight." Ward took one final look at the hard copy of the family's new principles and went to bed with the same feeling of accomplishment he had felt when he made a big play on the football field.

Develop Intimacy with Family

List the values and principles that your family mutually agree to live by. During what activities is your family acting at its optimal state and what avoidances need to be addressed?

We root our beliefs strongly in integrity, kindness, genuineness, caring, trust, honesty and responsibility. Our best moments come when we are together, in the moment, interacting, listening, understanding, and supporting each realm of each other's lives. We will prevent times when we are multi-tasking, arguing and disrespecting each other and/or his/her personal beliefs. We will act on our mission by focusing on: 1.) Spending time together. 2.) Defining and living our actions that always show integrity for each other. 3.) Working on group projects together. 4.) Planning trips and gatherings that ask for each other's input, suggestions, and guidance.

LIFEOGRAM

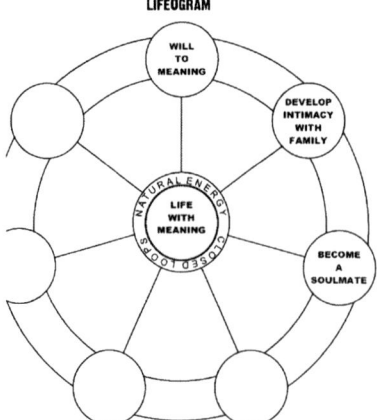

Hey, they have to live with you too.

LOOPS 4 *YOUR* LIFE

124

Develop Intimacy with Family

Summarize your principles in a brief description of what it means to be a member of your family.

Young Family – We are Young at Heart and in Name: Each member strives to maximize his/her personal development and add to the benefit of the family. Though we pursue our personal achievement, we understand that the strength of a family fosters a stronger individual, and stronger individuals build strong families. We will be individuals that have accomplished individual goals, but as a family we will be a stronger and greater force than any individual could even imagine. It is our responsibility to share our mission with other families in hopes of helping them reach our level of warmth.

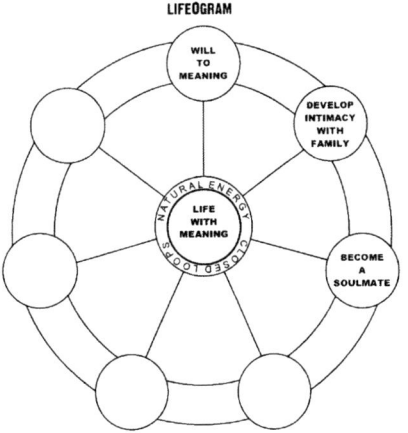

LIFEOGRAM

What are your family's principles?

LOOPS 4 *YOUR* LIFE

Chapter 32

A BETTER UNDERSTANDING OF A RELATIONSHIP

"Love is a verb. Love - the feeling - is a fruit of love, the verb. So love her. Serve her. Sacrifice. Listen to her. Empathize. Appreciate. Affirm her. Love is a value that is actualized through loving actions."

Steven Covey

That next morning woke Ward with a new energy, one he hadn't experienced in a long time. "Do you feel that?" Sophia asked.

"Yes, I feel like we have just overcome a huge obstacle and a burden was lifted from my back."

On a mission, the family was awake and back in the kitchen where breakfast turned into a team effort instead of a Sophia's chef special. Megan grabbed silverware and set the table. She then helped boost Steve onto the countertop to reach some plates. While Ward started cracking eggs, Sophia rinsed the vegetables. The team worked in perfect rhythm and breakfast was ready in minutes.

"Spinach and pepper omelets for everyone," Ward pronounced as he carefully filled everyone's plate.

Though the meal was clearly not as enticing as sugary cereal, Steve and Megan proceeded to sample bites of vegetables as they tried to focus on just the egg. Finishing nearly all of their meal, the kids were set off on their short walk to school with full stomachs and warm hearts.

"Have you ever seen the kids so eager to, at least, try vegetables?" Ward asked.

"I was thinking the same thing, Babe. I don't think that they found a new favorite, but their faces showed it tasted better than when we try to force feed them."

Setting his recent notes on the table, Ward sat down and happily noted, "You know, Ace has left us a great gift, and I have genuinely enjoyed the time we have spent the last couple of days."

Nodding her head, Sophia agreed, "It is too bad he isn't here to share it with us. He would be very proud of you."

"All of my other accomplishes were easily completed by myself, or with some of Ace's guidance. However, these latest loops take a group effort. His work is unfinished, and I am running out of clues. He has another loop, but there are no notes to back it up."

Sophia finished making a cup of tea and sat down beside Ward. She twisted the piece of paper that her husband was working on to the proper angle so she could read it.

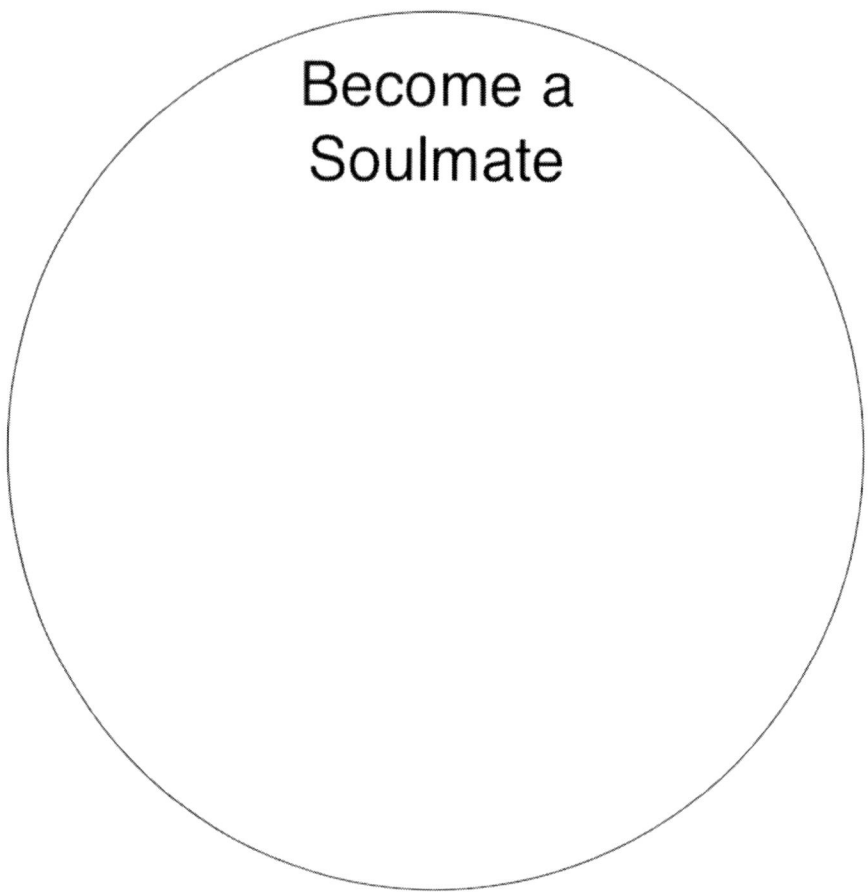

Become a
Soulmate

"Where do you think we should start completing this loop?" Ward asked.

"Has he ever mentioned anything about this or anything about his relationships?" his wife said trying to spark remembrance.

"No, he never said anything. Once he told me about a serious relationship he had, but he never said anything that sounded like advice. I don't think that he had any leverage to give advice on a subject in which he was lacking." They both sat quietly pondering the loop.

Sophia broke the silence with a suggestion. "Knowing Ace, he was probably very particular with each of his words. Let's break the phrase down in a little more depth. Become-A-Soul-Mate." She continued. "Maybe he meant to say Find-A-Soul-Mate. He probably has regrets in not finding…"

Ward cut her off. "He did say something. Yes, that must be what he was trying to say."

Sophia stood there confused. "What did he say?"

Her husband continued, "He said something about love being a thing you do instead of a thing you feel. He said it's not what Hollywood portrays it as. He was trying to explain this concept to me, but I was not getting it."

"That kind of makes sense when you think of it," Sophia stated. "It is the whole givers' gain thing right? You cannot expect something you have not given. You know, I watched a program on TV about that once. A marriage counselor said if you want to rekindle the fire in the relationship, you must do loving things for each other."

A light bulb went off in Ward's head. "Rekindle the fire. Yes, this is what Ace talked about. He said that he referred to his lost relationship as 'fueling the fire.' He said he stopped fueling the fire, and it went out. I bet he was going to say if a person wants to restart the fire, that person has to strike a match and start doing loving things."

The newly motivated husband and wife sat at the kitchen table nearly all morning writing their thoughts on the next loop. Finishing writing the last sentence, Ward said, "You know, I learned something today. Ace might have not been in any position to speak words of wisdom without hypocrisy as far as his relationship experience goes. However, sometimes you can learn just as much from a person who hasn't accomplished great tasks. If they can't tell you what to do, they sure can tell you what not to do. Had I been more open-minded, I would have picked up on this idea sooner. Committing an act of love can open your eyes to a whole new world. Only if you give love, as a verb, can you experience love, as a feeling. Ace once related a quote from Wayne Dyer, 'If you change the way you look at things, the things you look at change.' I now understand. I also think this is why the kids liked the breakfast this morning. Whether Steve and Megan liked the breakfast or not, it was much more edible since they helped and it was made with love." Sophia's face glowed with excitement, and she gave Ward a big hug.

Become a Soulmate

Love is something that you do. Love, the action, creates love, the feeling. What principles will you live by and for to perform loving acts and strengthen your relationship? What behaviors act in opposition and subdue love, the feeling?

First and foremost, we must cherish each and every moment when we are together and never be too busy to listen to each other. Arguments never create anything except hurt feelings. On disagreeing subjects, we promise to understand the other person's perspective and realize that there is no right or wrong, only different opinions. Loving gestures will be committed 'just because,' and they will genuinely be done without expecting anything in return. A relationship is not a 50/50 effort. We must each be willing to give 100% without anything expected in return. We promise to listen to each other with full attentiveness and understanding as the first time we talked. We can never learn too much about each other, and we will never know it all.

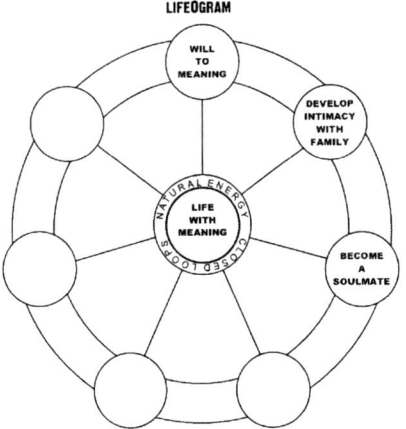

LIFEOGRAM

STOP

Looking in the same direction, together.

LOOPS 4 *YOUR* LIFE

Chapter 33

LEAVE IT BETTER THAN YOU FOUND IT

"There is nothing in a caterpillar that tells you it's going to be a butterfly." Buck Minster Fuller

When Ward returned to *The Saint's Kitchen* a week later, Zack gave a solemn look of understanding about his absence. In turn Ward matched Zack's look with one of assurance. Everything was okay. He was happy to be back at work. The fast-paced day quickly turned to evening, and Ward spent the majority of his time next to the statue of 'David' greeting customers at the entrance. As the night wound down, Zack handed Ward a piece of paper with some thirty names, numbers, and messages that had been compiled over the last week. Ward sighed, "I guess that's what I get for taking so much time off."

"Have fun!" Zack quipped as he scooted away. Looking down at the list, there was one message circled in red pen:

'Urban Mountain Realty (406) 560-3828 - He says it's important.'

"Hmm," Ward thought as he turned his head to the giant statue behind him. "What do you think, David? Should I give this guy a call right now?" Staring into the statue's eyes under the facemask, Ward smiled and said, "Well, you seem pretty confident about the whole idea. I think I'll call him immediately. Thanks for the advice!"

Dialing the number as he hopped into his car, Ward didn't make it ten feet home before the gist of the conversation forced him to pull over. He couldn't believe what he was hearing. "Hello, Ward, this is Walt Goldman." Stalled in the middle of the parking lot, Ward was speechless and confused that the same businessman/land developer who previously seemed so arrogant was apologizing and making an entirely different offer.

"Ward, I have thought about this long and hard, and we would like to fund the franchising of *The Saint's Kitchen* in all twenty-two of the new malls we are going to build. We will use different names to make them specific to each location, but we want to recreate the atmosphere and the kid's program. Kids have to learn to be smart off the field as well as on the field. Our locations will stretch all over the country from Seattle to Memphis!"

Thunderstruck, Ward grabbed the unfinished *loopOgram* from the passenger seat and began taking notes on the backside as Mr. Goldman continued talking, "I was on a vacation that took me from Yellowstone to Glacier National Park. When I was in Helena, I stopped by your restaurant again and fell in love with the new atmosphere and the food! You have truly transformed *Little Sicily* into something much greater than I could have ever imagined. *The Saint's Kitchen* gave me such a memorable experience I told my team we had to have the restaurant in every mall we build. They saw my enthusiasm and agreed. What do you think?"

Finally managing to find some words, Ward expressed his willingness to make the plan a reality, and they arranged the necessary preparations before finishing the late night conversation. "Wow" was the only word Ward could say to himself parked on the side of the road. "Wow, wow, wow! I used to think of Walt Goldman as a sleazy, Scrooge-like man. I guess everyone really does have a positive aspect within." Recalling Ace's final principles in the first loop, Ward repeated the coincidence to himself. "Ace noted that he would always find the good in every person and every situation, and now I see why."

If only Ace could have seen this turnabout, how proud he would have been. From three restaurants to twenty-five; Ward's business had finally reached the big time. The systematization efforts were really paying off. On top of that, he would be making substantial money. Each location of the restaurants would provide Ward, personally, with $50,000 a year, for yearly total of $1.25 million. By doing what he loved and creating his little sport-specific restaurant, he would be able to provide his family with all the finances they would ever need. Thinking about it, Ward realized he didn't even need to show up for work, and he would still generate substantial passive income. He had reached the final stage in the path to financial independence; financial freedom. With that freedom, Ward would have the time to do whatever his heart desired.

Ward finished his drive home, jumped from the car and ran inside. Though his high intensity had become somewhat of a trend, he still startled his wife. Sophia sprung from the living room, asking why he was out of breath.

For the next 15 minutes, Ward paced the kitchen explaining the call with Goldman, how his restaurants would be in 25 locations, and how their money problems were over. "Walt is actually a very kind man, Honey. Did you know that his company donates over $1 million yearly to youth programs over the entire states, and some of our programs in Helena have actually been funded by him."

Ward was ecstatic, but Sophia remained surprisingly stoic. "What are you going to do now?" she asked.

Taken aback by Sophia's' reaction, Ward responded, "Well, I'll still be manager and guide this big expansion, but... What's wrong Sophy? I thought you'd be happier about all this."

"I *am* happy Ward, and truly grateful. Conversely, will this new arrangement alone be enough to give your life its full meaning?"

Ward gave his wife a questioning look as she continued her questions, "What are you going to do with all your newfound free time? Are you just going to be a manager and owner for the next thirty years?"

Ward was starting to get irritated, "So, what if I were? I don't think that would be a bad life at all! What are you getting at?"

She asked, "What do your waiters ask their customers?"

Ward responded, "How can I serve you?"

She stepped forward, "Exactly! Though *The Saint's Kitchen* serves thousands of people an amazing dining experience, don't miss the opportunity to intimately serve another realm of people."

Ward shot back, "What are you saying? That I quit my job and join the Peace Corps or something!"

She grabbed his hands, "No, Ward. All I'm suggesting is that you have a gift; an awareness of life and how to make the most of it, and most people are not aware of this gift. Sharing it with those in need would fill your life with even *more* meaning. It's like how Ace's legacy lives on within you."

Ward was silent for a moment as Sophia's words sank in. "You're right. I wouldn't be where I am today if Ace didn't come and offer a helping hand." Recalling Ace's final letter to him, the words, "*You've given me more than you may ever know*" flashed across Ward's mind. "That's the fourth Loop! Ace found meaning in his life by leaving a legacy that continues to live within me!

LIFEOGRAM

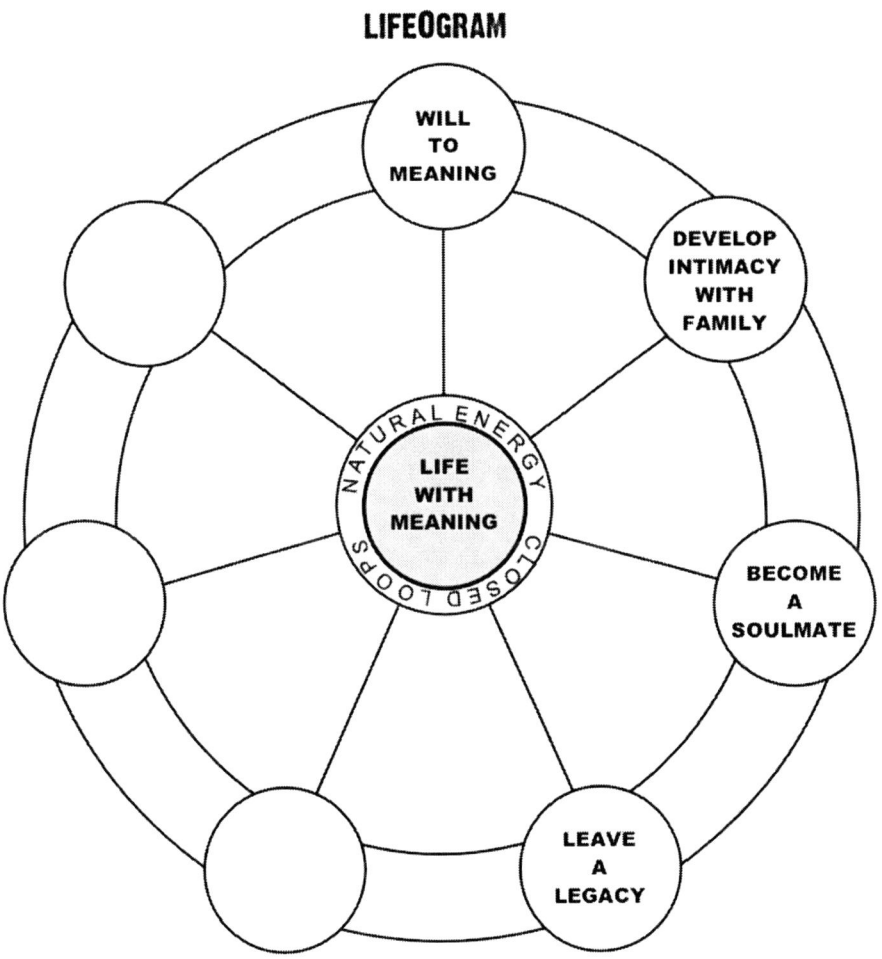

Leave a Legacy

Leaving a legacy fulfills a spiritual need to have a sense of meaning, contribution and purpose in life. How will you leave a legacy in accordance with your principles and passions?

I will leave a legacy in four different realms 1.) business 2.) family 3.) society 4.) daily grind. In the business realm, I will help Little Sicily grow while making sure we stay true to our vision. In family, I will strive to pass on the principles of closeness, kindness and integrity to our children. For the society realm, I will offer guidance and wisdom to help others discover their personal path to success and happiness like we did for me. In the daily grind, I will apply the code 'Leave it better than you found it'. Therefore, even if it's not my job to pick up a piece of garbage somewhere, I will because of my code. Leaving a legacy in these four unique ways will provide a balanced and fulfilling contribution to my life.

The more I make, the more I leave behind.

LOOPS 4 *YOUR* LIFE

Chapter 34

THE SEEDS OF AN IDEA

"If we change the way we look at things, the things we look at change." Dr. Wayne Dyer

The next month was a whirlwind of activity for Ward. There were many new projects to complete in preparation for his restaurant's nation-wide launch. With all the recent work, he was struggling to find time and wisdom to add other loops to his recent loopOgram. However, Ward still made time for his family. He went on a few hikes with Sophia. Megan and Steve made sure their dad was always present for the weekly board game. In addition, Ward volunteered as a counselor for a local summer camp for kids, one of the camps Mr. Goldman was so generous to support. He had a blast teaching seven-year-olds how to play all sorts of outdoor sports. The experience provided a whole new meaning to his life that he hadn't felt before. One day in particular, Ward, the chief counselor, was to lead a group of twenty kids on a hike up Mount Helena.

It was a beautiful summer day, with a sky immense of friendly clouds and soft winds. They made it halfway up the climb when one of the kids asked why so many trees had red pine needles. "My daddy said it's a shame for all these trees to die," a little girl added.

Pausing, Ward replied, "It can be sad to see so many big and majestic trees die. However, even as these trees die, new trees like this young quaking aspen are able to grow in their place." Seeing a good teaching point Ward continued, "It's a natural progression. Where once the big, old trees blocked new seeds from growing into new trees, their fall opens up the sky to the young saplings below. It's the natural cycle of life."

"Good work!" Ward thought to himself. "Sometimes I even surprise myself!"

Then with another burst of inspiration, he continued, "Who we are is a product of what we've thought about in our life. All the thoughts in our life have been little, tiny seeds. From those seeds, the thoughts we've chosen to 'water' or focus on, knowingly or not, are the seeds that become the big trees in the forest of our mind. So, if we always focus on the negative in situations that come before us, we water the seeds that say, 'I can't,' 'That's not fair,' and 'Why me?' Those thoughts become the big trees of the forest that make up who we become." Ward continued, half-speaking to himself as he looked from kid to tree, "If we water the positive seeds in our mind, when we meet the harsh challenges of life, we will say, 'I can,' 'I'll overcome this,' and 'How can I prevail?' Our thoughts shape us. Who we are can be found within those thoughts, along with who we will become tomorrow. Once planted, the key is knowing we choose, consciously or not, whether we will cultivate them, or whether they will wither!"

Ward finished his spontaneous revelation with a look around him. A couple kids were listening while the rest were trying to hide from him behind trees or by blending in with the brush. "Maybe a little too much for their age," Ward thought.

A little girl stepped up to Ward, "Counselor Young, can I lead the group for a while?" Regretting his answer almost immediately, Ward said, "Okay."

Immediately, the little girl went off the trail, through a thicket and over a tiny mountain stream. The kids kept right behind her, while Ward trailed the whole group. Not enjoying the lack of a plan, Ward raised his voice and asked, "Where are we going?"

The little girl turned around with a smile and said, "Nowhere."

"What? Why *nowhere*?"

She replied, "Why not!" and began marching again, leading the group of kids further off trail. Ward did his best to keep up, amazed the seven-year-olds were outpacing him. As he passed a big tree Ward saw all of them crouched around a three-foot wide hole in the ground. The fearless leader looked up and asked, "Can we go *in* there?!" For Ward (and any other person), the decision was a no brainer. Of course, they couldn't go in the cave! Who knew how deep it went, or what might be in there? Plus, something didn't feel right about the cave.

"I'm sorry, kids, but can we get back to the trail?" Despite a loud groan of disapproval from the group, they obeyed.

The rest of the trip was a blur, but Ward couldn't get the cave from his mind. Ever since he met Ace, Ward tried to keep an open mind to new ideas and nuggets of wisdom. Compared to the mind of a seven-year old though, he realized just how closed his mind had been. Of course, he couldn't put the kids into an unsafe situation, but it seemed there was something to learn from this state of affairs.

Coming home early in the evening, Ward related what happened during the hike and revealed his inner thoughts to Sophia. He talked about his revelation 'our thoughts shape us' and 'we reap what we sow,' Sophia added, "So, if we watch garbage on the TV all day, our thoughts start to become garbage! Garbage in, garbage out!" She smiled to herself. Ward then related the cave incident and how he felt he was missing the point. Sophia paused and replied, "Children sure have a beginner's mind, don't they? It's thirsty. As we get older, it seems we make more and more 'final decisions' and stop growing. We decide something is 'right' or 'wrong' and then we stop learning any further information about it. We say our way is 'right' and everyone else is 'wrong'. But if we concluded the world was flat and closed our mind to any other thought, we would be far from the truth!"

Ward injected, "Perhaps the best wisdom is to always look for wisdom...Honey, could you grab the Loop-o-gram?"

LIFEOGRAM

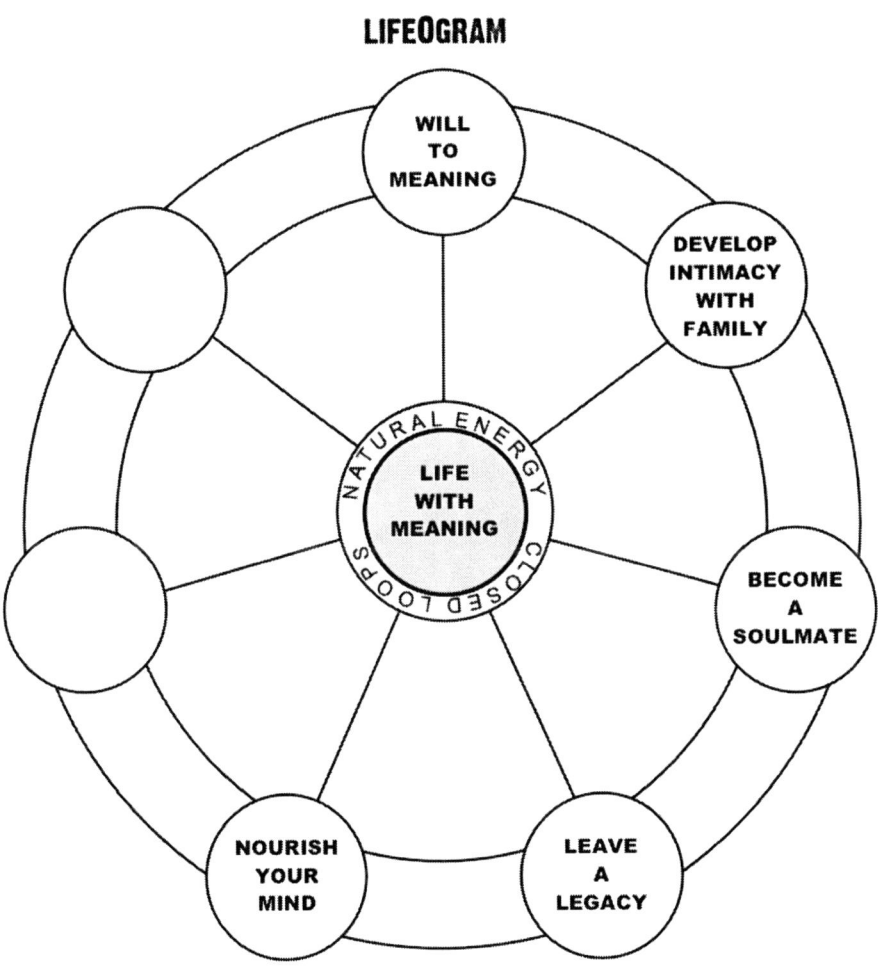

Nourish the Mind

Since our thoughts shape who we become, it is essential that we surround ourselves daily with positive influences. This will allow good thoughts to be sown and fulfilling results to be reaped. Keeping a beginner's mind will allow us to find wisdom in even the smallest of everyday events. How can you be more open-minded and keep a beginner's mind?

I will become more aware if I have a closed mind to an idea or situation before me, and I will strive to open it to find any wisdom that may be present. There is wisdom in every situation, and I will make it a habit to ask myself the question, 'What can I learn from this?' I will cut down the amount of TV shows I watch at night, and use that time for myself and my family even more.

 Always expand yourself. The opposite of growing is wilting and there is no in between.

LOOPS 4 *YOUR* LIFE

Chapter 35

FREEDOM!

"Men look for retreats for themselves… Yet all this is very unlike a philosopher, when you may at any hour you please retreat into yourself. For nowhere does a man retreat into more quiet or more privacy than into his own mind."   Marcus Aurelius

"Wow, only two more loops to go!" Sophia said as she leaned over Ward's shoulder.

"I know. This has been quite the ride." Ward replied.

Then Sophia questioned, "Is it necessary to find seven loops? I mean, what if you can only find five? Seven is just a number."

Pausing for a second, Ward concluded, "I do realize seven is just a number. Then again, there is something very magical about this loopOgram, and I plan on sticking to the diagram that has already taught me so much. I am determined to find seven loops, and I will not rest until that day comes." A supportive hug and kiss on the cheek came from his wife.

Later that evening, the family spent time playing cards together and talking about the school day. Once the kids went to bed, Sophia and Ward decided to put in a movie. "What movie do you want to watch Honey?"

"How about "Braveheart?" I still haven't seen it."

He nodded his head, "I forgot you haven't seen it! In that case, it is definitely time to learn about the *First War of Scottish Independence!*"

The last time Ward watched "Braveheart" he was a junior in college. He had given a speech on William Wallace and the topic of freedom. Unexpectedly, the movie brought up the painful memory of his poor speech in World History and his failing the class. As the movie neared the climatic ending, Sophia saw that Ward's eyes were moist. She pretended not to notice.

It was past midnight when the movie ended. "I really liked it!" Sophia stated, trying to induce a conversation.

Ward was slow to reply as his eyes returned from far away to focus on his wife. "Yeah... It seemed to have a different meaning than I remember..." He continued, "Last time I watched "Braveheart," I thought it was sad how William Wallace was never able to taste the freedom he helped to create. This time, however, I realized he was free the *whole time!*"

Sophia responded, "Another Loop?"

"Maybe." Ward replied. He was feeling the lateness of the hour and finished by saying, "Let's sleep on it."

That night, Ward had a dream. In a dark, enormous cave, he was following a silent herd of bodies down deeper into the cave. They were all slowly and softly moving lower and lower down the cavern. One step at a time, the bodies in front of him seemed to sway in unison, left and right, left and right, down and down. Suddenly, a bright light to Ward's left caught his attention. One body was moving against the masses in the opposite direction. Ace! Although he didn't have a torch, his body emitted a natural light. Like William Wallace, his face was painted with blue paint. Ward called out to him but there was no reply. Ace easily seemed to glide past the herd as he moved towards the cave entrance. Ward turned around, but the bodies behind him kept pushing him further and further. He managed to break free and started to pursue Ace's illuminated body up the cavern. He tried to catch up, but somehow Ace kept expanding the distance between them around each bend. Suddenly, the exit to the cave was within sight and Ward started sprinting to catch Ace. He was closing in. Only a few yards away, near the exit, Ward grabbed for Ace, but his mentor's body disappeared in the blinding light of the outside.

"Ward! Are you okay?" It was Sophia. "You were talking in your sleep and you're all sweaty!"

Half awake Ward mumbled, "Things are not what they seem," as he fell immediately back asleep.

When Ward awoke in the morning, Sophia had breakfast and the unfinished loopOgram sitting on the table next to the bed. "I thought you might be on to something," she said. Ward proceeded to relate his eerie dream. "Tell me, how does your dream relate to a life with meaning?" she asked.

"It's *Freedom,* Sophia. But the secret to freedom is that it comes in more than one form. The more forms we have, the happier and more meaningful our lives can become."

Sophia asked, "Have you figured out what these forms are?"

Ward answered, "I think so. I think there exist four forms of freedom."

Recalling his World History class and the speeches on freedom reminded Ward of the foreign exchange student from Kyrgyzstan. "The first form of freedom is one that we take for granted because we were born into it. It's our social/political freedom. In many other cultures and countries, the rights of the citizens are suppressed. There was a girl named Albina in my World History class who spoke about her own path to freedom. In her culture, women didn't have the social and political rights we take for granted. Albina discussed how her dad arranged for her to be married through the tradition known as 'bride kidnapping.' She had no say in the matter and would not have known about the arrangement except for her sister overhearing the conversation. Luckily for Albina, she was able to escape to a land which allows for much more social and political freedom."

"What's the next one?" Sophia asked.

Ward took a drink of water and continued. "The second form is financial freedom, which we've experienced recently with the success of *our business*. What financial freedom means is being free from *having to* work just to get a paycheck. The meaning of being financially free isn't being able to buy new toys. The true meaning is having time to do what you want and to live as you desire. Many people who work hard and achieve higher forms of financial freedom find they have more time to help others; like my volunteer work with those kids."

Smiling, Sophia waited to hear more. Ward continued, "The trap that happens to many people once they acquire money is that they stop doing *anything*. Since they don't *have to* work to survive, they simply stop working at all. They become sloths and laziness rules their lives. Sooner or later they lose their unique human spirit, and often their money too! So, the key is to work toward one's personal level of financial freedom, the level where they feel financially liberated to do whatever they desire."

Sophia added, "And it seems to me, that many people who *do* have financial freedom devote more of their focus to giving back to others."

"I would definitely agree." Ward replied.

Looking outside, Ward pointed to a bird singing in the tree. "See that bird. She's happy to be exactly where she is, whistling in the tree. When I went hiking yesterday with those kids, my goal was to make it to the top of Mount Helena. When I let that little girl lead, I asked here where she going, and she simply said, 'Nowhere.' When I asked 'Why,' she replied, 'Why not?' I admire that perspective because it means you are *free* from the outcome. You can enjoy the present moment fully without worrying about the finish." Ward continued, "It's like going fishing. The happiest fishermen don't go fishing with the sole desire to catch a giant fish. Sure, that's one of their hopes, but the happy fisherman goes fishing to enjoy the moment he has with nature." Ward paused, "That is the third form of freedom: freedom from outcome, the ability to enjoy the now."

"So, what's the fourth form of freedom?" She asked.

"How about I eat this omelet first before it gets any colder?" Ward said with a wink as he grabbed a fork. As Ward ate his omelet, Sophia took the opportunity to write down the morning's revelations so they wouldn't be forgotten. Just as Ward swallowed the last bite, Sophia asked again to hear the fourth form of freedom.

"This fourth is the most difficult freedom to possess, but just like the third form, the ability to enjoy the now, it is available to *anyone* if they work towards it! The fourth form of freedom comes when we free ourselves from other people's opinions and our Ego." Ward began to explain, "Those kids don't seem to care what anyone else thinks of them. However, as we grow, we lose the freedom that comes from innocence.

We start to define ourselves by what we have, what we do, and by what other people think of us. Freedom from other's opinions isn't lost forever, however. As we mature and gain a greater understanding of our surroundings, we have to replace that lost innocence with newfound wisdom." Pointing to his head Ward continued, "A wisdom that recognizes the only opinion that matters is the one we have of ourselves."

"That is easier said than done," Sophia said.

"Yes, I agree it is", said Ward, "but that's how we can free ourselves from the cave of darkness called Ego. In that cave, everyone chases material desires in unending darkness, always hurrying to obtain more and more materials so they can achieve happiness one day. In the cave, we define ourselves by what we have, what we do, and what other people think of us. Therefore, our happiness and meaning in life are out of our control. We enslave both within the cave of darkness. However, when we choose our own path from the cave, like Ace led me to in my dream, we choose to free ourselves from those meaningless desires. We find a more fulfilling life waiting for us at the cave's exit, illuminating and liberating our spirits!"

Ward fell quiet. His partner was also silent before responding, "That's really deep, Ward. I've never considered freedom like that before. This one is definitely the sixth loop!" They huddled around the loopOgram and wrote.

LIFEOGRAM

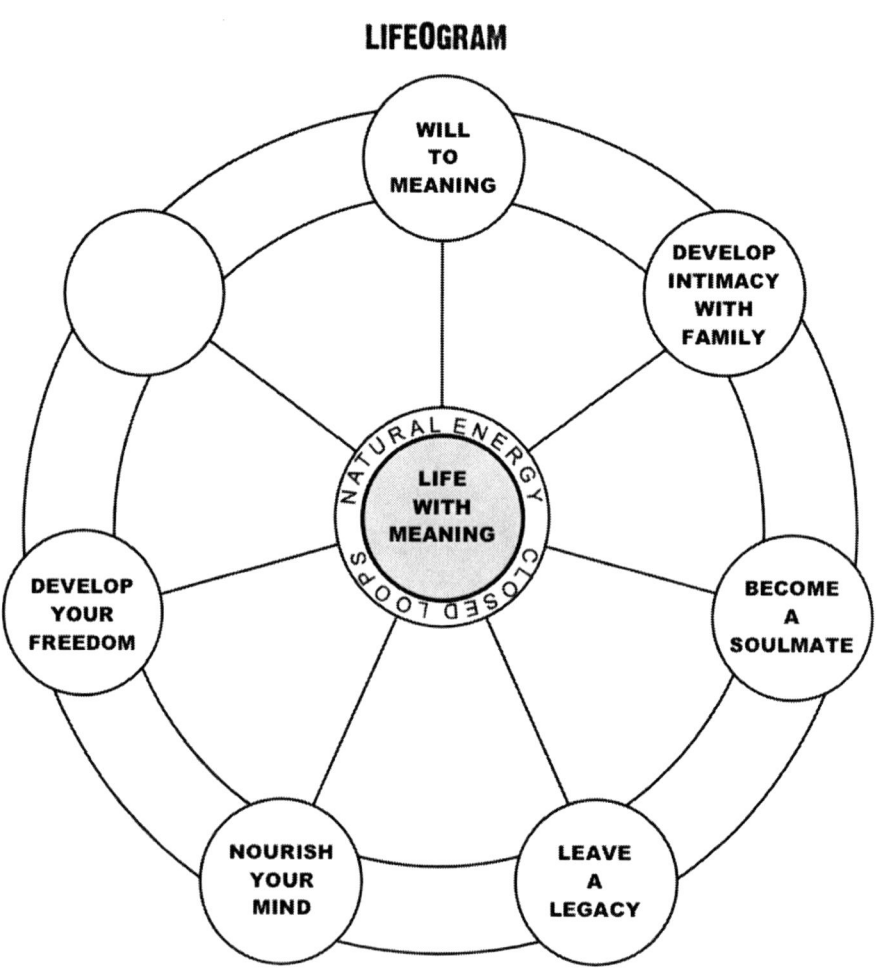

Develop Your Freedom

Freedom comes in four basic forms: 1. Social/Political Freedom 2. Financial Freedom 3. Freedom From Outcome 4. Freedom From Ego. Freedom isn't something that is just handed out. It must be earned, practiced and cultivated. How will you continually instill all four forms of freedom into your life?

1.) I will remind myself of how grateful I am to live in a country with many social and political freedoms. I will cherish and respect the freedom of those people with whom I interact.

2.) I will continue to educate myself on how to manage my money financially. Money can cause much sorrow and/or much happiness. Understanding how to manage it deserves my attention.

 You have to become a winner on the inside before you can be one on the outside.

LOOPS 4 *YOUR* LIFE

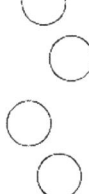

Develop Your Freedom

Freedom comes in four basic forms: 1. Social/Political Freedom 2. Financial Freedom 3. Freedom From Outcome 4. Freedom From Ego. Freedom isn't something that is just handed out. It must be earned, practiced and cultivated. How will you continually instill all four forms of freedom into your life?

3.) I will focus on the present moment and enjoy it fully. As opposed to worrying about things that are in the future or out of my control.

4.) I will remind myself that I am not my job, my house, my car or what other people think of me. I know who I am and what I stand for. I will remain true to myself regardless of any given circumstances.

Can you be proud without being arrogant?

Loops 4 *YOUR* Life

154

Chapter 36

WHERE IS THE FINISH LINE?

"There will come a time when you believe everything is finished. That
will be the beginning." Louis L'Amour

A full grin encompassed Ward's face the entire day at
work. He was so pleased with his newfound wisdom that he
couldn't wait to get home and to start work on the project
again. Immediately upon returning home, he compiled the
latest loops he had discovered, adding them to the loopOgram.

"Only one more loop to go Honey."

LIFEOGRAM

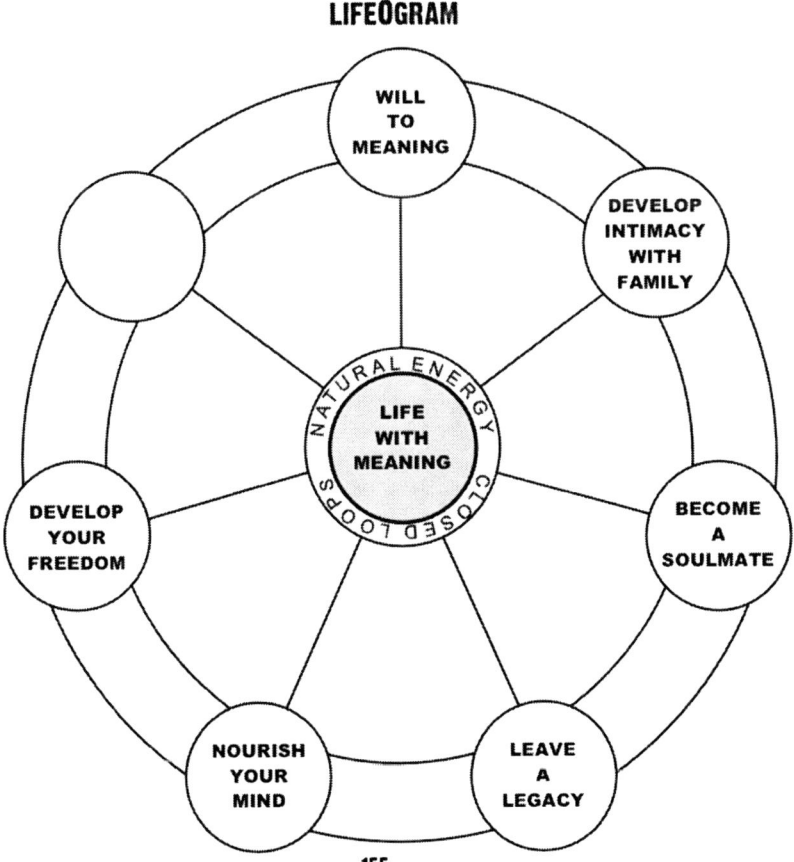

Smiling at her husband, Sophia calmly suggested, "Are you sure you need to find seven? I mean, I understand where you are coming from, but I just think maybe this project is good with six."

Pondering only for a slight second, Ward responded, "I've thought about this long and hard, and I would not be doing Ace justice if I stopped here. I just know there is more to the project, and it will be amazing when it is finished."

Sophia kissed him on the cheek, "I will support you 100% either way. I feel that we have grown so much closer as a family since this project has started, and I don't want it to end. It's like Ace has left you a mystery message from the grave, and curiosity excites me each time you discover a new lesson. I will be here to help in the morning, but I am going to get a good night's rest tonight."

Sitting at the kitchen table, Ward pondered for hours, unable to get the slightest idea where to start the next loop. Every last conversation with Ace ran through his head, and every recent experience he could imagine. Still nothing could spark that fire. He even put a chair in his closet, and turned the lights off to eliminate distractions, as he would often do to concentrate. People had called him weird many times for sitting in a dark closet, but he had mentioned that many great thinkers got their ideas from similar places. He called it 'The Edison Room.'

When morning came, Sophia was surprised to see Ward not in the bed. She wandered around the house unable to find him anywhere. His car was outside, but he was nowhere to be found. Megan and Steve were running around the house looking when they both screamed so loud they fell over. They had opened the door to the closet and their dad, who was asleep in the chair leaning against the door, fell from the chair tumbling into the hallway.

"Did you sleep in there the whole night?" Sophia asked trying not to laugh.

"I guess so. I must have just zoned out trying to figure out where to start this next loop. Nothing seems to come to mind."

His wife assured him, "Just give it some time. An idea will come to you soon. You can't expect an answer overnight."

While days passed, Ward's mind grew more blank the harder and harder he thought. Days turned into weeks, and he just couldn't seem to get even the slightest hint at another lesson. Though his project might have been unfinished, he was very pleased with his family's progress so far. They were truly living their virtues, and each family member was improving his/her personal development daily.

Though his life had improved since he started the project, he was over-stressed. It had been four weeks of lost sleep and high stress, and Ward contemplated giving up. He then justified his decision as he walked to his car, "It is not like I am giving up. I'm just prioritizing; I am not going to try and force an answer. I'll just let it happen."

On the drive home, he called his wife. "Hey Sophy, I have just concluded that I am not going to stress over this anymore. I am grateful for what I have gained, and I'm going to be more present and live the principles we have declared."

On the other end of the phone, his wife replied, "That's nice. Sometimes you just need to not over think things. It is usually when you stop trying so hard that the answer just appears."

At that instant, Ward looked out the window and saw a boy in his mid-twenties sitting on the corner of the street with a cardboard sign in his hands. "I will be home in twenty minutes Honey, I have something to do really quick." He pulled his car over and stepped out. While Ward had never been the kind to give money to beggars, he believed he could help the boy out in another way.

As Ward approached the panhandler, he could see he was very strong and capable of work, but his body was tired from scrounging. The restaurant owner cleared a spot on the grass and sat next to the man. "I'll tell you what. I am completely against giving money to beggars, but I am 100% for giving out opportunities. I am not sure what your story is, but if you really want to make some money, I can offer you a job at our restaurant." He then handed the man his card. "If you show up here tomorrow at 8 A.M. we could really use a strong hand to help at the loading dock. If you prove to be a good worker, I promise to help you, in any way I can."

Without the slightest hesitation, the man stood and said, "Yes, Sir. Thank you so much. I don't want to be begging for money, I just don't know what to do. I am a good worker, I promise."

As Ward returned to his car, he added, "I bet you are; I will see you in the morning."

Ecstatic, the boy walked Ward back to his car. "Thank you so much; this offer is better than money."

The appreciative look made it obvious no one had ever shown the boy so much attention and that he had never been so grateful, in his entire life. As he sat back down in his car, Ward grabbed the beat up manila envelope from the passenger seat, and handed the boy a tattered piece of paper. "This goalOgram changed my life years ago, and I have no doubt that it will change yours too. Bring it with you tomorrow and we will begin to rebuild your life."

The restaurant owner reached out and shook his hand, "Glad to help. My name is Ward Young."

Looking him directly in his eyes, the boy replied, "I am Ace Collins."

With that said, warm memories of his old mentor lit Ward's face. "I used to have a friend called Ace. In fact, it is because of what he taught me, I have the kindness to help you today. I'm sure you will do much in your life. Ace is a great name."

With a thankful grin still on his face, the boy replied, "I hope I can live up to the name. I was named after my father. His name was Ace too. I never met him, but my mother said he was a great man."

A tear fell from Ward's face as the realization sank in. That very instant, when he tossed the envelope back on the passenger seat, Ace's note fell out. For the first time, he recognized writing on the back of one of the diagrams that he had never before read. It was as if Ace was present that very moment, thanking Ward for his good deed with the final loop. Progress Your Success!

Progress Your Success

Success is specific to each individual in that current moment of time. There is no accomplishment of greater or lesser value than any other. Each success is just a spoke of equal significance in the 'wheel of life'. What is of vital importance is that you continually strive to better yourself every minute of every hour of everyday. Accomplishments are merely checkpoints in a larger journey, and whether you win or lose is of little importance compared to learning and progressing forward. Stagnancy is a step backwards.

What have you learned from your previous successes and what gives your life meaning? Declare the principles that you want to guide your life and die by them. (list them below & use more paper if necessary)

Sign Your Name Here:

LIFEOGRAM

WILL TO MEANING

DEVELOP INTIMACY WITH FAMILY

PROGRESS YOUR SUCCESS

NATURAL ENERGY

LIFE WITH MEANING

CLOSED LOOPS

DEVELOP YOUR FREEDOM

BECOME A SOULMATE

NOURISH YOUR MIND

LEAVE A LEGACY

STOP

Enjoy each step forward.

LOOPS 4 *YOUR* LIFE

161

THE COOL-DOWN

It's been said that *happiness* isn't the real goal in life, but that *growing* is. Each of us feels that the growth of our society depends on us being a better person today than we were yesterday and better tomorrow than we are today. Along those lines, Dr. Denis Waitley once told us, "You don't write a book once you've made it, you write a book to help you make it." We have grown immensely from the writing process, expanding what we thought would be a short book on goal-setting into a book encompassing much of our life's philosophies. Through the process we have truly *Progressed Our Success.*

THE LOOPS PHILOSOPHY & THE LOOPOGRAM

Since the discovery of television and more recently, the Internet, we have been continuously swamped with a non-stop stream of information. For any question we have, the answer is supposedly a click away. Consequently, the most profound wisdom from years past barely receives a response from us today. It's barely worth our time!

When people try to teach us something, our response is usually something like: "Thanks, but I already know that." The irony of such thinking is, we probably do... to some extent.

However, it's one thing to know a matter *intellectually*, and quite another to know it *emotionally* and *experientially*.

Today, we think we *know* countless subjects, but we don't really *know* them until we *experience* and *feel* them. It's not until a nugget of wisdom sinks to the bottom of our mind, heart, and soul that we can mine it for its true value. Until it reaches that point, we simply do not know it at the deepest levels. Emotional understanding makes all the difference.

The *Loops Philosophy* concerns knowing a few powerful principles extremely well instead of allowing millions of competing thoughts to swamp the mind, thus numbing our focus and slurring thoughts. The loopOgram is a powerful tool to help organize your thoughts and guide you to a fulfilling life. Over the past few decades, 'mind mapping' has grown in popularity and for good reason. It allows for creative, uninhibited brainstorming. However, when it comes to living our lives by specific principles, we need a map with consistent structure. The loopOgram is a map with structure, and the hidden benefit is that the more you use it, the more beneficial it becomes. It provides clarity and structure to the most complex of issues. Paraphrasing Henry David Thoreau:

> *A single step doesn't make a trail on the earth,*
> *and a single thought won't make a trail in the mind.*
> *To make a deep trail on the earth, we must walk it*
> *again & again. To make a deep trail in the mind, we*
> *must think over & over the kind of thoughts we wish*
> *to dominate and empower our lives.*

By using the loopOgram for our personal and professional lives, we create deep mental trails we know well and thus allowing us to walk with more vitality.

MORE ON LOOPOGRAMS

The loopOgram is comprised of three parts. The more you become familiar with the format of the loopOgram, the more powerful it becomes.

The outer seven circles of the diagram, called the *Essential Loops*, must be closed to accomplish your centralized goal or objective. The trapezoid-like shapes on the outer ring are called *Fundamental Building Blocks*, and they hold the loops together acting as extra support.

Within the circle there are also seven more points that resemble pieces of a pie called *Behavior Habits*. It is vital to practice and utilize all twenty-one points and to understand their application. This book, *Loops4Life,* focuses on the *Essential Loops.*

The *Essential Loops* are the foundation to this structure. They are a great starting point and must all be acted out. Each step, at times, may fall subsequent to another. However, the beauty with our system is that it is not linear. You may start anywhere at anytime. However, each loop is interdependent upon each other. You cannot forget about a loop after it is closed. Just like in life, you must remember the fundamentals.

Moreover, the *Fundamental Building Blocks* are the traits that you must express to fulfill the *Essential Loops*. Develop these traits until they form into habits. Recall each building block from time to time and evaluate your actions.

Finally, the *Behavior Habits* are the specific ways to act to develop your *Fundamental Building Blocks* and close your *Essential Loops*. Think of the loopOgram as the blueprints for your life. Anytime you hit rough spot, refer back to the loopOgram and it will help you get on track and get you back in line.

Our mentor and co-author, Dr. Mike Chaet, was the creator of the loopOgram. More information about The Loops Philosophy can be found in the book he co-authored with our friend, Steven Lundin, *Loops- 7 Keys to Small Business Success*, published by McGraw Hill. Steve, the best-selling author of the widely distributed FISH books, has also been a very helpful advisor to this project. We also encourage you to refer to the website www.loops4biz.com and www.loops 4health.com. Mike can be contacted at mike@loops4biz.com. Steve can be contacted at steve@loops4biz.com.

PAY IT FORWARD

One of the best ways to truly understand a subject is share what you have learned with someone else. With that said, if you enjoyed the book, pay it forward and spread the word. Make a stand today, and start your own goalOgram. Log onto loops4biz.com/templates.php to download your FREE loopOgrams. Then, let the *Progression of Success* help you achieve your goals in all stages of life.

MIKE CHAET, PH.D.

a.k.a. "The Club Doc," is a bestselling author and founder of CMS International, the fitness industry's largest consulting firm. A lecturer, author, and consultant, he has been involved in the development and management of over 2,500 clubs and small businesses worldwide. He currently splits time in Bozeman, MT and Phoenix, AZ with his wife Mary and little black pug dog, Ozzy. He may be contacted at mike@loops4biz.com.

LEARN MORE

To find out more about the *Loops 4 Life* program, the L4L workshop, or powerful speaking engagements, email us at books@loops4biz.com.

If you wish, you can learn more about us at our personal websites: www.garretgarrels.com and www.nickmilodragovich.com.

Loops 4 Life

350 Janet St. Condo 1B

Helena, MT 59601

CPSIA information can be obtained at www.ICGtesting.com
Printed in the USA
BVOW010027180512

290534BV00007B/7/P